The Manual
of
Social Media

Manoj Pandey

ABOUT THIS MANUAL

[The second edition]

The Manual is meant to be a treatise on social media as it exists today, covering all related aspects and yet in a concise volume. It deals with different facets of the subject, starting from the definition and other basics to history, technological concepts, its sociological importance and likely future.

The second edition is thoroughly revised, with the latest data and other updates. Social media has affected and been affected enormously during the COVID-19 pandemic during 2020-21. Recent elections the world over have been highly divisive, and social media is seen as a 'partner in crime'. Such developments necessitated a more detailed discussion on crisis communication and misinformation.

Historical facts have been taken from available resources and cross-verified. However, since there are different versions for some of these, such facts are subject to correction or further elaboration in future editions.

The book deals with different aspects of social media in different chapters, but many of them tend to overlap with each other. For example, shady political tweets may have been discussed in chapters on the use of social media in elections, social media influencers and fake social media content. To avoid repetition, I have tried to deal with a repeating concept/ example in one place and cross-referenced it in other places.

A great deal of information based on data-mining, surveys, scholarly studies and expert observations on social media is available on the web. To keep the Manual short, I have given only a few examples, just to support the discussion at that place.

ACKNOWLEDGMENTS, DISCLOSURES, DECLARATIONS

The Manual is being published in my personal capacity, and the views expressed in it have nothing to do with my official functions or any organization or government office I may be associated with in the past or at present.

The information, statements and advice contained in the Manual are of general nature and the expressions used may not be legally binding and, as such, are not meant to be used for legal purposes.

References and other links to various websites or other resources are not a certificate from me.

Examples of product/ service providers (e.g. web hosts, search engines, online picture sharing websites) are given at various places. Inclusion of such references or their comparatively higher placement in a list does not signify a recommendation or certification of quality, nor does exclusion or lower placement signify a poor opinion about the product/ service/ firm.

Website addresses provided here are those of global websites; some major firms have local servers in many countries and the addresses given here may be automatically directed to those local websites when opened by the reader and may have different content.

Web references may be taken as retrieved in February 2021. Some of them may have been edited later.

Another book of mine, *The Manual of Blogging*, finds reference in many places because blogging is a part of social media and many relevant topics have been discussed in greater detail there, and not with the intent to promote that book.

I respect the individuality of each gender. However, for the sake of easy reading, I have used the common noun 'he' and its derivatives to include all genders.

STYLE AND FORMAT

I have given meanings of technical terms and jargon when they first come for discussion so that the reader uses the intended meaning out of many possible.

Many new expressions have originated, meanings of some earlier expressions have undergone change and some have reached the level of jargon in the web lingo. Since there is no standardization about how they are written (e.g. webhost, web host, web-host; site-map, sitemap), the most commonly used expression in US English has been used in the Manual.

In absence of established words or better expressions in the dictionary, some derived expressions have been used in the Manual, e.g. *commenter*: one who comments on a blog or elsewhere on the web; *searcher*: one who makes a web search; *upvote*: to give a positive vote; *spammy*: behaving like spam.

URLs have been provided along with web references in square brackets, especially when they come for the first time. Major sources have been given in the <u>References</u> chapter, and where applicable they have been referred to in the body of the Manual with their placement in the list of references.

The language used in the Manual is US English.

CONTENTS

Key features of free blogging platforms: Blogger – Wordpress - LiveJournal – Tumblr – Medium - Postach.io

Other blogging platforms - Website builders - Content Management System (CMS) - Earning from blogging

TECHNOLOGICAL ASPECTS RELATED TO SOCIAL MEDIA

SOCIAL MEDIA BEYOND PERSONAL SOCIALIZATION

Use of social media for business, earning: How social media helps businesses - How social media-savvy businesses actually use it - Social Media Platforms Best Suited for Businesses - Monetization by social media platforms themselves - Social Commerce - How do individuals earn through social media - Social Media Influencers - Content, social media and inbound marketing

Use of social media in democratic politics and elections - What purpose does social media serve during elections - How politicos use social media - Whether social media really makes an impact on election outcomes? - Aberrations in the use of social media in politics and elections - Efforts by social media platforms towards free and fair elections

Use of social media by governments - Governments' handling of social media as an adversary - Governments' use of social media for providing information and services

Social media adoption by non-profits - Social media and activism

Use of social media in formal education - Edublogging - Social media in formal research

Use of social media in crisis communication

CONCERNS RELATING TO SAFETY & SECURITY, PRIVACY AND GOVERNMENT CONTROL

Privacy and security concerns over conduct of social media platforms: Privacy concerns - Privacy versus public good - Privacy obligation of publishers on the web - Unsafe technology - Toxic content on social media platforms

Indiscretion and carelessness by social media users

Child safety on social media

Government control

SOCIAL MEDIA AND CRIME

How social media users unwittingly become partners in crime

LEGAL ASPECTS RELATING TO SOCIAL MEDIA

Important laws that directly relate to social media users - Freedom of expression - Intellectual property rights - Attribution and disclosure - Privacy rights - Defamation and libel - Criminal laws

IMPACT OF SOCIAL MEDIA ON INDIVIDUAL LIVES AND THE SOCIETY

The sociology of social media - Does social media make people happy? - Social media impacts well being - Social media when someone does not want it - Social media after one's death - Social media influences opinions - Physical & mental health issues associated with social media - Online abuse

COVID-19 and social media: Actions taken by major social media and other tech platforms during COVID-19 - Institutional initiatives and social media - Consumption of social media during the pandemic - Qualitative aspects of social media communication during the pandemic

SOCIAL MEDIA IN DIFFERENT LANGUAGES

Social media in languages other than English - Breaking the language barrier - Is English swallowing other languages due to social media? - Social media's influence on languages

SOCIAL MEDIA AS MASS MEDIA AND MEDIUM OF FREE EXPRESSION

Social media and the freedom of expression

Misinformation and fake news: The making and spreading of fake news - Impact of fake news on individuals, society and systems - Action against fake news on social media

GLOSSARY

REFERENCES

DEFINING SOCIAL MEDIA

Social media needs to be properly defined so that we know exactly what we are talking about.

However, in defining such a dynamic expression, we should be conscious that its definition may change according to context; and due to fast developments in web technologies, the definitions as they stand today may not last many years.

Let us start with the definitions of social media given by some prominent web dictionaries:

- Websites and applications that enable users to create and share content or to participate in social networking: Oxford dictionary

- Websites and computer programs that allow people to communicate and share information on the internet using a computer or mobile phone: Cambridge dictionary

- Websites and other online means of communication that are used by large groups of people to share information and to develop social and professional contacts: Dictionary.com

- Forms of electronic communication (such as websites for social networking and microblogging) through which users create online communities to share information, ideas, personal messages, and other content (such as videos): Merriam-Webster dictionary

The essence of social media, as may be seen from the above definitions, is **distributed creation of content, content sharing** and – most important - **online socialization**. Socialization includes collaboration in content creation, response to others' content and networking among account holders.

There may be a difference of opinion whether to include all web 2.0 websites in the social media net, but the concept, more than a technical definition, is what should matter, and a loose definition given above (in bold) perhaps captures the sense of *social media* the best.

Depending upon which of these three activities (distributed creation of content, content sharing and socialization) is in focus, social media entities can be grouped as follows, allowing groups to overlap with others:

- Social networking platforms
- Social content sharing sites
- Social bookmarking sites
- Microblogging sites
- Instant messaging platforms
- Question-answer sites
- Wikis
- Blogs

WWW, WEB 2.0 AND THE SOCIAL MEDIA

Let us see where social media fits in today's digital world and what features distinguish different types of digital/ web media.

Web technologies are growing in many directions, and many new functionalities have emerged that were earlier not possible (e.g. instant interactions and notifications using JavaScript and other scripting languages, CSS-based beautification of sites). These unforeseen developments have led to a sudden emergence of new platforms rather than earlier platforms gradually getting mature. They have also led to overlap among all types of platforms with varied functionalities, and people confusing between the terms that define them.

Let us start with the broadest of all terms relating to digital content. All new forms of content distribution as compared to traditional forms such as the print press, radio and television and modes of content sharing through portable devices, are often referred to as **new media**.

The new media encompasses the entire **World Wide Web** (WWW) and includes other digital media (e.g. digital television).

Let us be clear that WWW is not internet. **Internet** is the technology that connects computers and smart devices and makes it possible for them to talk to each other. The World Wide Web is the information or knowledge part of this global network of inter-connected computers. All types of websites are part of the WWW.

A big part of WWW is passive, one-way. Most traditional websites just serve information, and it is for the visitor to visit and read/ view the information. At most, there could be a facility for giving feedback or a bit of sharing the content. On the other hand, in the last two decades, starting with closed networks, blogs, bulletin boards and forums, more and more of the web has become interactive and collaborative. It encourages sharing of content and social engagement. This is what is called **web 2.0**.

Web 2.0 is a general expression, unlike specific versions of software that are denoted by numbers (e.g. Windows 10, Firefox 58.0, Android 11.2).

Social media is the main constituent of this web 2.0 and the two terms are nearly synonymous. As listed above, it includes social networks, blogs, chat sites and so on – entities that have distributed content creation, content sharing and socialization at their core.

Much of today's social media is platform-driven and the user's web page is not an independent entity. The user must create an account with a social media platform, and all his activities and data are stored with the platform. This enables instant sharing of messages with others on the same platform.

All things considered, social media is also a form of distributed **mass media** (The term mass media refers to the communication systems that broadcast news and information, and traditionally includes newspapers and magazines, radio and television). In fact, social media entities can broadcast information faster and more extensively than many older forms of mass media. Besides, while the traditional mass media is mostly passive and commercially oriented, social media is more democratic and open; it also often includes more shades of opinions than the traditional media. We would further discuss this aspect of social media in <u>Social Media as Mass Media and Medium of Free Expression</u> chapter.

SOCIAL NETWORKING

Social networking is that part of social media in which *networking* is the key activity. The focus is on creating one's profile on the platform and making a network (of community members, friends or followers), publishing one's posts, making quick comments on others' posts, and liking and sharing the content on the fly.

Social networking is mediated through platforms specially created for networking. The major social networking platforms include *Facebook* [https://facebook.com] and *Twitter* [https://twitter.com]. Most of these platforms are free.

The content on social networks is mostly in short form, and sharing and commenting are instant. The original content and responses are seen by others in the network, thus leading to an expansion in sharing and engagement.

BLOGGING

Blogging, in its simplest definition, is the **distributed creation and sharing of long-form content on the www**. This, however, is a very narrow definition of blogging, and people use the term to include all forms of creation and sharing of content on the web. You could do video blogging on YouTube or can call your Facebook account/ page as your blog.

When blogging started, blogging was high on social networking but that role is now played by social networking and sharing platforms.

Technically, blogs are websites that contain standalone web pages, called *posts*, which are added over a period. Thus, a blog in its most elementary form is like a digital diary containing posts that are stacked one upon the other, the latest being on top. Blogs usually allow sharing of posts on social media and commenting on them.

Blogs can be standalone websites or can be opened on blogging platforms, which are free or paid. *Blogger* [https://blogger.com] and *Wordpress* [https://wordpress.com] are the most popular free blogging platforms. However, blogs can be highly sophisticated and can take the shape of huge websites with many functionalities. In fact, some big news portals that started as small blogs still call themselves blogs. *HuffPost* [https://huffingtonpost.com], *Mashable* [https://mashable. com] and *TechCrunch* [https://techcrunch.com] are among huge blogs.

MICRO-BLOGGING

Micro-blogging refers to blogging (regular posting, in reverse-chronological order, with commenting facility, etc.) of very short content.

Twitter [https://twitter.com] and *Sina Weibo* [https://weibo.com] are the most popular micro-blogging platforms. Twitter started with the limit of 140 characters in one post but in 2017 raised it to 280 characters. *Tumblr* [https://tumblr.com], a blogging platform that is known for small posts and easy sharing of others' posts, is also considered a micro-blogging platform.

SOCIAL SHARING

Social sharing sites are websites that focus on sharing of content. The content is user-generated and is shared widely over the network of users on that platform.

While social *networking* and other social media sites too share content, the focus on social networks is on community-building; content is usually not a 'brand' in itself. On social *sharing* platforms, people visit to find a type of content, usually from a known content creator, and promote and share it if they like. *Instagram* [https://instagram.com] and *Pinterest* [https://pinterest.com] are popular image-sharing sites while *YouTube* [https://youtube.com] is the most popular video sharing site.

SOCIAL BOOKMARKING

Social bookmarking is parallel to bookmarking of content on printed books and internet browsers: when you like a piece of content, you place a tag on it to mark it as important. On social bookmarking platforms, a piece of content that is published elsewhere is served and people respond to it in different ways (e.g. voting up or down, liking or disliking, commenting) and share it with others. Thus, these sites act as search engines and curators for content based on users' interests.

Digg [https://digg.com], *Mix* [https://mix.com] (earlier StumbleUpon), *Reddit* [https://reddit.com], Scoop.it! [https://www.scoop.it] and *Flipboard* [https://flipboard.com] are popular bookmarking sites.

INSTANT MESSAGING

Instant messaging and chat platforms are the ones on which people share information on a real-time basis, mostly on their mobile phones. The focus is on the quick sharing of information and quick response to it.

Instant messaging can be called a new, more functional and more social form of *chatting*. The two terms have become almost synonymous.

Instant messaging has grown and is growing at a scorching pace. Private messaging and small groups are stated to be the fastest-growing segments of online communication in 2020.

The major instant messaging platforms include *WhatsApp* [https://whatsapp.com], *WeChat* [https://wechat.com], QQ [https://imqq.com] and *Telegram* [https://web.telegram.org].

OTHER WEB 2.0 FORMATS

There are a number of variations of the social media entities mentioned above, and hybrids of myriad type come on the scene now and then. Depending upon how much value people find in them and other factors such as their financial muscle, some of them become mainstream and some disappear. As detailed in <u>History of Social Media</u> chapter, dozens of them have disappeared fast and some ruled the scene for some time and then vanished.

Please note that the categories of social media mentioned above are not sacrosanct. Many social media categories overlap, as social media platforms have some common features or they add new features over time.

There are other web formats that are 'social' but they lack the socialization offered by social networks and instant messengers. They do have some features of social media, e.g. they generate content through users, allow people to respond and react to others' content, lead to the development of groups/ communities around them, and so on.

The following are some web 2.0 formats that do not fit in the categories mentioned above:

Forum is a website (or a section of a website) organized into different topics on which users can post messages and reply to others' messages. Though they originated differently, web *forums*, *bulletin boards* or *discussion boards* are usually taken as synonymous.

Usually, the topics are arranged tree-like. A topic has sub-topics that in turn may have further branches.

Forums are generally accessible to all but posting is limited to registered users.

Question-answer sites cater to queries on different topics. *Quora* [https://quora.com], *WikiHow* [https://wikihow.com], *Askfm* [https://ask.fm] and *Yahoo! Answers* [https://answers.yahoo.com] are popular Q-A sites.

Wikis, a special form of websites, are for sharing knowledge. In most cases, individual wiki pages can be written and edited by anybody with a registration on the platform.

Wikis have a unique way of arranging information on individual pages and the whole platform. Some of the common features of wikis include indexation of information, cross-references, social editing and validation of information, and citations.

Wikipedia [https://www.wikipedia.org] is the most popular wiki platform and acts as an enormous web encyclopedia. *Wikimedia* [https://www.wikimedia.org] is a group of content-rich educational wiki platforms.

Chat rooms are a more closed way of group communication but can sometimes be open too. Twitter allows users to create Twitter chats on different topics by using a hashtag (#).

Many tech/ social media platforms such as Google, Facebook, YouTube, Instagram, and Tumblr allow **live streaming** and simultaneous commenting. Periscope [https://www.periscope.tv] is a full-fledged video streaming app. During COVID-19 pandemic, people needed to keep in touch remotely with near and dear ones as well as office teams. Video conferencing, video streaming and webinar became mainstream, making the existing apps/ software very popular and leading to birth of new apps. During the pandemic, the popularity of live videos surpassed even the overall demand for video content.

There are several platforms that allow **communities** to develop around common interests or cater to existing communities. *Blackplanet* [https://www.blackplanet.com] caters to the black Americans. *Classmates* [https://www.classmates.com] connects alumni of different US schools. *Meetup* [https://www.meetup.com] encourages meeting like-minded people and making groups around a common interest. *Docquity* [https://docquity.com/#] is a network of doctors. *Godinterest* [https://godinterest.com] is a religious social community of Christians. *Ticco* [https://go-ticco.co] is a paid social network for professionals of AEC (architects, engineers and construction) and related areas. *Poetizer* [https://poetizer.com] is a social network of people interested in poetry. *Litopia* [https://litopia.com] calls itself a 'colony for writers'. *Academia.edu* [https://academia.edu] is a community of research scholars and publishes research papers that can be shared freely. *HARO* [https://www.helpareporter.com] and *MyBlogU* [https://myblogu.com]

are communities that help people get writing ideas, help in writing projects and promote others' writings.

Tinder [https://tinder.com] is a mobile app (also with an online version that came later) that connects people with similar interests. It is supposed to be the most used dating site, and has a number of account options. It introduced *swiping* to like or dislike other users on the platform. *Bumble* [https://bumble.com] is a 'female-first' dating app. It now has a fork for business socialization too. *Peanut* [https://www.peanut-app.io] is an app that connects mothers and promotes close physical engagement. Dribble [https://dribbble.com] is a platform for design professionals. And the list goes on!

Webinars (seminars on the web) have been a medium of serious discourse beyond social media. However, COVID-19 has made them commonplace by adding new features of interactivity and socialization, which bring webinars into the social media fold. Existing professional webinar providers (e.g. Webex: https://www.webex.com) have been joined by new ones (e.g. Zoom: https://zoom.us and Livestorm: https://livestorm.co), some of them providing free services for small groups. Earlier video-calling offers from tech platforms (e.g. Google, WhatsApp) have also introduced social media features for **video conferencing** and online meetups.

Online gaming is not social media but latest multi-player online games share some features of social media, such as engaging, generating content and sharing data with others. In many games, there are in-build interactivity features other than gaming *per se*. In addition, social media is getting integrated with games as most people now play online games on smartphones. One estimate says, nearly 3.5 billion people around the world play online video games today, with three-quarters of them playing games on smartphones.

Virtual world is yet another form of online environment in which people engage with one another and share data. A virtual world is a computer-simulated reality with scenes in which people participate by assuming a virtual *avatar*. There is a big overlap between virtual worlds and multi-player video games, but virtual worlds can have applications beyond gaming.

HISTORY OF SOCIAL MEDIA

The history of social media is quite interesting. The advent of personal computers (PCs), internet, mobile phones and apps have contributed successively as accelerators, even disruptors, towards invention of new technologies. Earlier technological limits on the amount and speed of data exchange were also successively broken by new developments in information and communication technologies (ICT).

From sharing of files on computers through physical means to instant content sharing and communication, the pace towards the creation of social media was rather slow. However, once blogs and social networks took birth, there was no stopping social media.

We can divide the history of online communication and social media into these 4 distinct phases:

- Up to 1997 or so: No or limited availability of PCs and internet; start of digital networking with lots of limitations. Online chat/ instant messaging starts getting popular.

- 1997 to 2002: Blogging emerges; *Six Degrees*, *LiveJournal*, *GeoCities* and other online societies gave the taste of things to come.

- 2002 to 2006: *Friendster*, *LinkedIn* and *Myspace* rule the social media.

- 2006 onwards: The advent of *Facebook* and *Twitter* on the social media scene leads to the downfall of many established platforms. New social platforms with focus on visual content, e.g. *Instagram*, become popular; new instant messaging apps such as *WhatsApp* connect the world real-time.

INITIAL PHASE OF SOCIAL MEDIA

ARPANET (Advanced Research Projects Agency Network), a US Defense Department funded project was the first network of computers that used *packet switching* technology – thus making it possible to have multiple simultaneous communications through the same channel as against the *circuit switching* technology used by telephone networks. The concept of socialization was yet years away but this technology, and later the TCP/IP protocol that too was adopted first by ARPANET, laid the foundation of connected computers or internet.

The concept of computer networking was taking shape in the 1960s in different research institutions, and finally the ARPANET network took shape in 1967. By 1969, ARPANET had a directory of connected computers. ARPANET led to 'social' interaction among researchers though much limited in expanse and content: while the main content was to be in support of government business, some personal messaging was allowed, but the of the network for commercial purposes was considered anti-social and illegal.

Simultaneously, other research institutions were engaged in developing their own small-scale networks for information exchange. ARPANET itself changed hands and grew away from defense.

In the 1970s, *bulletin board systems* (BBSs) started appearing in some major American cities. In Berkley, a public bulletin board called *Community Memory* started in 1973. If you were in its neighborhood, you could access the Community Memory server through its terminal in your locality and get information on different matters. BBSs improved with upgrades in technology and allowed file transfer. You could log on to the host server and use the BBS to communicate, and download games and movies. BBSs declined fast in the mid-1990s as internet and WWW became mainstream.

Another important player in the evolution of online communication was *Compuserve*, a company that – besides dial up and other communication services – provided text messaging in the late 1970s and 1980s. *Prodigy* and *AOL* were other major BBS providers of that time.

In 1979, Tom Truscott and Jim Ellis conceived the idea of *Usenet* at Duke University, and in association with Steve Bellovin of Carolina University they made the first Usenet program. In Usenet, users could post messages on a particular topic of common interest (called *newsgroup*), on UNIX servers, using a Unix-to-Unix Copy (UUCP) network architecture. The initial idea was to upgrade the bulletin board style announcement system of universities and have a better exchange of views on different topics.

The importance of Usenet has gone down considerably, but it still is a way for exchange of information. At present, *Giganews* [https://www.giganews.com] is the largest Usenet service provider.

Usenet and its contemporary, the bulletin board systems, were precursors to *message forums* of later days. With the arrival of internet, these forums gave way to *internet forums*. Forums have been very popular, especially in technical and other professional spheres.

In 1983, with the adoption of the *TCP/IP protocol* for communication among computers, the modern **internet** was born. The possibilities opened up, not only for communication between the chosen few computers but computers at large across the globe.

In 1985, General Electric started a network for exchange of information, *GENie* (General Electric Network for Information Exchange). It offered games, shopping and mail, and had forums too. At its peak, it had about three hundred thousand users. It could not survive when graphics-based online services were started by AOL and Prodigy and also for commercial reasons.

AOL also came up with *AIM* (AOL Instant Messaging), which made instant messaging popular in the US. Also came *Yahoo Messenger*, *MSN Messenger* and *ICQ*. They retained their popularity for over a decade before succumbing to the onslaught of *Google Chat* and then modern social networking platforms, especially *Facebook*.

Tim Berners-Lee, working on a project at CERN in Switzerland, had in the 1980s conceptualized the idea of sharing information/ data across internet, and in 1989 came with the idea of creating a database of information and sharing it through hypertext links – thus arose the idea of a **world wide web** of information. The *WWW* actually came into being in 1991.

In 1988, *Internet Relay Chat* (IRC) was invented by Jarkko Oikarinen at the University of Oulu, Finland, to replace a BBS. IRCs continued to operate until the early years of the 21st century. If you had the IRC software on your computer, which provided server-client communication, you could connect with the server and other connected clients and have chat with all of them. IRCs were used for chatting as well as for file sharing and link sharing. IRCs' chatting applications can be called the fore-runners of modern-day instant messaging apps.

Once the WWW was in place, many platforms with the provision of online socialization emerged. *GeoCities* came in 1994 and *Classmates* in 1995. On GeoCities, the third most visited website in 1999, you could open your own web page that looked like your personal website. The pages were initially grouped according to real cities or regions, hence the name. The platform closed down in 2009 except its Japanese version that too stopped functioning in 2019. On Classmates, you could initially only search for old classmates and interact; later, it added many socialization features.

Simultaneously, after the advent of the World Wide Web, the normal HTML web pages started being used in technical circles for updates on topics and events. Swarthmore student Justin Hall's *Justin's Links from the Underground*, started in 1994, is regarded as the first personal **blog**.

Scripting News by Dave Winer was a professionally created website for disseminating technology news as well as his ideas and versions of the programming world. This acted as an inspiration for many bloggers and thus helped greatly in the growth of blogging in its early days.

The term *blog* came after many blogs were already in existence. In December 1997, Jorn Barger coined the term 'weblog' for 'logging the Web'. The word 'weblog' was dissected into 'we blog' and shortened into 'blog' by Peter Merholz in his blog *peterme.com* [http://www.peterme.com] in April 1999.

Notably, the expression *social media* was first used in 1994 but it did not catch up. From 1996, expressions such as 'computer-supported social networks', 'virtual communities' and 'social networks' started being used with similar connotations.

THE SECOND PHASE OF SOCIAL MEDIA

The five years starting 1997 gave a new meaning to online socialization.

Six Degrees [http://sixdegrees.com], created in 1997, can be called the first social networking platform in today's terms. On it, you could create your own profile, add friends, and publish on forums. You could create your social group, which could expand to the next level – the levels going up to six, hence the name of the platform. Six Degrees was very active for about three years and then declined. It still operates as an 'invite only' social network.

Many other platforms arose and died down. *MoveOn* [now https://front.moveon.org] came in 1998 as an email group to collect petitions for opposing the impeachment of the US President, Bill Clinton. It later became a medium for promoting activism on other issues and now has a network that promotes collective social and political actions by citizens.

At least three big platforms tried to build communities based on racial affiliations and subsequently upgraded them with modern networking tools. *AsianAvenue* [now AsianAve: http://www.asianave.com] was started in 1997 and became popular in raising racial matters in the backdrop of the 1998 Winter Olympics. *BlackPlanet* [http://blackplanet.com], a network of black people started in 1999. *Migente* [http://www.migente.com] was opened in 2000 as a social network of the Hispanic community. All these platforms are still active.

In the field of **blogging**, in addition to individual blogs, a number of blogging platforms took shape in the mid-1990s and offered registration to common people. Bruce and Susan Ableson started *Open Diary* in 1997 as a blogging platform where one could open an online diary and interact with other community members. It was in existence till as late as 2014.

Blogs provided a mechanism by which people could freely jot down their life events and express their opinions, and also receive comments from visitors. Having one's own place on WWW and interaction through comments made blogs highly 'social' by the standards of that time. *Live Journal*, *Blogger* and *Xanga* came in 1999, and mainstream blogging took wings. Many free blogging platforms came in later years and some are taking birth even now. If you are interested in details on the history of blogging, you may refer to *The Manual of Blogging* [ref 55].

In 2000 came LunarStorm, one of the first commercial advertisement-financed social networking websites. It became highly popular among teenagers in some European countries but lost user count drastically after 2007 and was shut down in 2010.

Ryze [https://www.ryze.com], a popular business/ professional networking, came in 2001.

Wikipedia took shape in 2001 as a sort of online encyclopedia on which people could add and edit content. A collection of wikis on all conceivable topics, it continues to grow.

THIRD PHASE: SOCIAL MEDIA BUZZ ALL AROUND

In 2002-3, as computers were becoming more common and so was internet, and as the technology for instant dispatch and display developed, huge possibilities of social interaction on the net arose.

Friendster came in 2002 and became an instant rage. It can be called the first major social networking site. It also became a popular dating and social gaming site of that time. You could discover friends and friends-of-friends, thus grow your network. The platform closed down in 2015 as its users flocked to more modern social networks like Facebook and its gaming community started thinning.

MySpace, a hugely popular social networking site, came in 2003. On MySpace, you could fully customize your profile, and place multimedia on your account. That made it very popular among the youth, and it ruled the social media scene during 2005-2009. It later added instant messaging function too.

Hi5 was another major social networking platform that came into being in 2003. It also allowed customization of *profile* and different levels of friendship. The platform [https://secure.hi5.com] is still active.

2003 also saw the launch of the blogging platform WordPress, which subsequently grew into the world's most used content management system (CMS) for building websites and blogs.

LinkedIn [https://linkedin.com], the most popular and influential business social media site of today and XING [https://www.xing.com], another such platform came in 2003.

LastFM came into being in 2002. It was one of the first online music databases and online radio streaming.

In 2003, photo-sharing sites ***Flickr*** [https://www.flickr.com] and ***Photobucket*** [http://photobucket.com] took birth. Both are quite popular and active even now and have added many features in recent years.

SecondLife [https://secondlife.com], a multi-player online gaming platform, also came into being in 2003. It now has a buzzing community and a virtual reality platform too.

Following the high growth of social networking and blogging, social bookmarking sites emerged during 2003-5 and became a force to reckon with. ***Del.icio.us*** [https://del.icio.us] came in 2003, ***Digg*** [http://digg.com] in 2004 and ***Reddit*** [https://www.reddit.com] in 2005. These sites allowed users to bookmark the content on the web if they liked it, tag it to different keywords, vote it up or down, comment on it and share it with others easily.

In 2004, many more social media entities took shape, including *Facebook* (its Harvard version), *Orkut*, *Multiply* and *Ning*. *Multiply* focused on privacy and security. *Orkut* had very good socialization features and had two redesigns in the following years. It was very popular in Brazil and India before Facebook annihilated it. *Ning* [https://www.ning.com] came as a CMS that allowed one to set up one's own social network within this platform, without much technical knowledge. Later on, it became a paid service and now runs in the same avatar.

Squidoo came in 2005. A very popular content-sharing site that paid writers for making their content-rich pages or *'lenses'*, it died down in 2014.

YouTube [https://youtube.com], which today is the biggest video sharing platform, began its operations in 2005.

In 2005, Yahoo! came up with *Yahoo! 360⁰*, a blogging platform with social sharing and networking features, but closed it within four years. It allowed users to shift to *Yahoo! Blog* but that too was closed down in 2013.

Bebo [https://www.bebo.com], another platform that came up in the same year, even overtook Myspace in the UK. It saw a massive decline after the advent of Facebook, was re-launched in 2015 and is now focused on video streaming.

FOURTH PHASE OF SOCIAL MEDIA: SOCIAL NETWORKING BECOMES PART OF PEOPLE'S EVERYDAY LIFE

This is not a distinct phase in chronological sense, because after 2003-4, new social media entities have been taking shape, and some appearing and disappearing every year.

What makes 2006 a milestone year in the journey of social media is the start of ***Facebook*** [https://facebook.com] and ***Twitter*** [https://twitter.com].

Facebook was already in existence for nearly two years but it was made public in 2006. Soon, it overtook all other social media platforms and is at present the biggest social network.

Twitter also came in 2006 and has been a sort of monopoly in the micro-blogging sphere all over the world, except in China. For a decade, it limited its posts, called *tweets*, to 140 characters and in 2017 raised the tweet character-limit to 280.

Tumblr [https://tumblr.com] and *FriendFeed* came into existence in 2007. Tumblr's socialization features included micro-blogging, community building and anonymous blogging. Anonymity made it especially popular among the youth and teens. *FriendFeed* was a real-time feed aggregator from social networks and was closed down in 2015.

Several platforms and sites emerged in 2008-12 and beyond and many of them were lost in the crowd. Some tried integration between different platforms, some used GPS (geo-positioning system) based services, some were built for media sharing and streaming. They are so many in numbers that it will not be possible to list names of even the major ones, so let me just give some examples. *Posterous* came in 2009 as a simple blogging platform that allowed sharing of content on other platforms. It is no longer active. *Vine* [existing as https://vine.co] came in 2012 as a video micro-blogging platform, with the provision to host and share videos of up to 6-second duration. It went into 'archive state' in 2017. In 2010, Google offered *Google Buzz,* a social networking and messaging tool through Gmail and then expanded it as a platform, but within about a year, closed it down on privacy concerns and to offer a better product, *Google Plus.* Google Plus came in 2011 with a bang, made a number of changes over the years and finally was taken down in 2019 in favor of an enterprise version. Pheed came in 2012 with the promise of giving multiple sharing options (text, photo, audio, voice notes, video and live broadcasts) to users on a pay-per-view basis. However, it could not survive beyond 2016.

The following platforms that came during this period have survived and are doing well. **Spotify** [https://spotify.com] came in 2008 as an audio streaming platform with thousands of music tracks. **SoundCloud** [https://soundcloud.com] came up in 2007 and was made public in 2008 as a music sharing site. Today, it is a major audio distribution platform. **Foursquare** [https://foursquare.com] came in the same year with location tracking around the world and has had many versions since then. Today's popular image and video sharing platforms **Instagram** [https://Instagram.com] and **Pinterest** [https://pinterest.com] took birth in 2010 and **Snapchat** [https://snapchat.com] in 2011.

With the rising popularity of smartphones, most of the existing social media platforms started issuing their mobile apps. These led to even more instant communication and the availability of social media all the time, everywhere. The ones that came up after 2010 started with their mobile versions; some did not release their desktop versions at all. The use of GPS and the availability of fast internet on smartphones has taken us to a stage when social media is dictating not only our social lives but our personal, family and official/ business lives too.

As of 2021, social media is the biggest activity that people on the planet willfully do beyond the essential biological activities such as sleeping. It has also gathered a number of controversies relating to data theft, privacy intrusion, political bias, social networks not doing enough to check crimes, also concerns about loss of health and real-life socialization due to its excessive use. We shall discuss these concerns in the following chapters.

We are perhaps at the peak of the biggest wave of social media development and online social engagements *so far*, and are waiting for it to fall before a technological disruption takes us to a completely new wave – likely a new paradigm.

THE FUTURE OF SOCIAL MEDIA

The information and communication technologies (ICT) develop in all possible directions, and not all the new technological developments can be included in the sphere of social media. Social media would include only those technologies that have an element of content creation, content sharing, engagement and socialization. Thus, new entities for broadcast (one-way communication to many), data sharing, utilities and tools for performing various functions, etc. have come up with the help of new ICT technologies but are not necessarily *social media*.

Major changes in technology give new choices to consumers whose expectations too keep growing with every new offer. Some developments break barriers of distance, knowledge and language. Some make the earlier tasks much easier. These necessitate a constant change in hardware and component designs, and in turn development of a new range of devices. Software development as well as hardware designing and production need high sums of money. So, very fast growth in business and also overnight bankruptcy take place due to changes in technology and consumer preferences.

ICT also has a history of surprise inventions that lead to disruption of an existing line of evolution. For example, when pagers became mainstream around the 1980s, they were thought as the ultimate devices through which you could send instant messages to people without them having a wired telephone. However, the technology was overwhelmed within a few years by mobile phones.

Blogs gave a very new experience to the world in that anybody could have a website, broadcast himself on the web and instantly interact with his readers. In terms of engagement, blogging has now given way to platform-based social networking and social sharing.

Forums, chat rooms, camera on mobile phones, smart devices, e-commerce, social networks, instant messaging apps, mobile money, bitcoin, augmented and virtual reality, and internet of things – they all have given us newer experiences that were not imaginable some years back except in science fiction. Some of these have changed the ways in which technology was expected to evolve. For example, when floppy disks were in use, it was thought that their sizes would keep reducing while storage space would increase. Then came CDs that erased floppy disks from the scene and all the investments made by companies making them turned sour. CDs were soon replaced by two types of DVDs and then came pen-drives and portable hard drives with capacities a million times of floppy disks.

Talking of disruption, there already are many forks of technology that look promising, rather imminent. One area that may soon see a paradigm change is the way social media is controlled; already an open (as against proprietary), cross-platform tech specification for social networking, *OpenSocial*, has been evolved and is in use. This and similar technologies may soon allow for distributed control of social networking.

Another development worth a mention is the TTC protocol. This decentralized networking protocol is trying to challenge the centralized social networking in which a single platform controls all content, interactions and money power of the network. TTC uses *blockchain* technology for introducing transparency, anonymity and security of content on a social network. The contributor (content creator as well as one active on the network) is rewarded for its action by way of tokens, which act like cryptocurrency. It is argued that this system incentivizes creators of quality content and active users rather than the company running the social media platform.

The talk of emerging alternative forms of social media will not be complete without the mention of *Mastadon* and similar other 'open social networks', which are not owned by corporations and hence not liable to too much control by governments. Mastadon [https://joinmastodon.org] is an example of such micro-blogging platforms. These can even talk to other similar systems, using a tech protocol, called *ActivityPub*.

Mastadon runs like a universe of independent communities, each looking like a Facebook Group. These communities are called 'instances' and can be hosted by any person or organization. People join instances based on their interests. Instances can talk to other instances too. People on such social networks are assured of non-algorithmic and ad-free feed.

There is also a talk of alternative forms of internet evolving, though none has taken shape yet. A parallel or much improved internet might completely change the way we engage online.

5G mobile technology is expected to bring about new forms of content, interactivity and technological integration.

These were just some illustrations of how a new concept can suddenly break the sequential developments in the field of technology.

It is not possible to predict the path of ICT and the products and services that arise out of them, even by top experts. Yet, the following major general trends are noticeable in the social media arena, and these may hold good for at least a couple of years if there is no major disruption.

- In the short term, much of the change in COVID-19 induced changes in social media consumption will stay. These include reliance on social media for alerts and news, and its rising use in business and institutional communication.

- The use of video on social media will rise fast because of greater availability of higher bandwidth, higher space in devices, ease of creating videos, and their inherent appeal vis-à-vis text, images and audio. Video streaming is also likely to grow fast.

- There will be enormous data sharing, facilitated by the availability of higher bandwidth and user demand.

- Highly immersive and integrative new technologies such as AR (=augmented reality), VR (=virtual reality) and IOT (=internet of things) will enter social media.

- Because of unseen privacy intrusion and data theft, people will become virtually naked. There is likely to be greater control of social media by governments and legal agencies, both covert and overt. Tools of tracking and identity theft in the hands of authorities, espionage networks and criminals might hurt the safety and security of individuals, societies and nations.

- New forms of mental and physical health issues would come up due to excessive and improper use of social media as well as devices. New branches of medicine will evolve to cope with these issues.

- As internet reaches underprivileged segments of society at a fast pace in the coming years, the use of social media by people not exposed to evolutionary stages could lead to an onslaught of misinformation, poor-quality entertainment and e-commerce/ social commerce on them. This can raise citizens' expectations and cause frustration with poor governance, resulting in serious social and political consequences in poor, ill-managed countries.

- Despite the challenges that social media poses, it will keep giving value to the life of people. That includes giving more choices for entertainment, better delivery of social messages and citizen services, and use during emergencies and disasters.

SOCIAL MEDIA IN NUMBERS

Firm numbers relating to social media are very difficult to assess because social media is highly distributed, massive and dynamic. Social media research firms make their assessments based on inputs from big social media platforms, their own tracking bots, statistical assumptions and other means. Therefore, we find a lot of variation in data from different sources. I have collated public data from some big sources such as Statista [https://www.statista.com], WeAreSocial [https://wearesocial.com], Pew Research Center [https://www.pewresearch.org], DataReportal [https://datareportal.com] and some more, and presented here.

Please note that even the most resourceful data-crunchers cannot arrive at precise figures because of sheer numbers, anonymous access, multiple sharing of messages and other such activities that are difficult to measure even with sophisticated bots and analytics tools. For example, it is argued that though Twitter numbers look smaller than many other social media platforms, the actual numbers could be much more given the sharing of tweets on instant messaging apps, and users accessing them without needing to log in to Twitter.

Let us group the available data into sections for its better appreciation.

HOW BIG IS SOCIAL MEDIA GLOBALLY?

As of early 2021, there are 7.84 billion people on the earth. Out of them, 4.8 billion have internet access. Out of them, 4.14 billion are active social media users and the number has grown very fast (about 13%) in 2020, aided by COVID-19 pandemic. Going by this data, the active social media accounts represent 53.6% of the global population. Since most social media users have more than one accounts, the number of actual users might be less. On the other hand, since only people above a certain age (usually 13 years) are eligible to open accounts on social media platforms, above two-thirds of the eligible population might be on social media.

Though social media covers almost the entire globe and the absolute number of social media users is huge, a large number of people are still not using social media at all, pointing to a global *social media divide*.

Of the active social media users, nearly 99% use smartphones for accessing social media.

It is reported that apps are the most used method of accessing social media, yet a good number of people use web platforms to access social media, including social networking sites.

The COVID-affected year 2020 saw growth not only in new users joining social media (nearly 2 million joining every day), but also the time spent on social media. On average, people use 15% of their waking time (equal to 2 and a half hours per day) on social media.

Number of social media accounts per person

People use more than one social media platform and also can have more than one account on the same platform.

On average, social media users have 8.4 accounts though all may not be active. The countries with the highest average number of accounts per social media user are as follows:

- India: 11.4 accounts per person

- UAE: 10.7

- Indonesia: 10.5

- Saudi Arabia: 10.4

- Mexico: 10.2

REGIONAL USAGE OF SOCIAL MEDIA

The highest penetration of social media is seen in the Americas: Northern America: 69% and Southern America: 68%. East Asia (which includes China and the Philippines) also has high social media penetration. The lowest penetration is reported in Africa and Central Asia.

Though internet and social media penetration is low in some regions, there are more social media users in these regions than even North America because of the sheer population in those regions, as can be seen from the data on distribution of social media users among geographical regions.

The data shows the percentage of global social media users located in different regions, in July 2020:

- Eastern Asia: 29.6%

- Southeast Asia: 13.4%

- Southern Asia: 13.1%

- Northern America: 9.2%

- South America: 7.6%

- Central, Western Europe: 5.5%

- Western Asia: 4.4%

- Southern Europe: 4%

- Eastern Europe: 3.3%

- Northern Africa: 3%

- Western Africa: 1.5%

- Eastern Africa: 1.2%

- Central America: 0.8%

- Northern Europe: 0.7%

- Southern Africa: 0.7%

- Australia, Oceania: 0.7%

- Caribbean: 0.6%

- Central Asia: 0.4%

- Central Africa: 0.3%

- Social network usage by country

The following data shows the number of users of social networks in the top 5 countries. Actual users in 2020 end and projected for 2025 are shown in millions:

- China: 926.84 - 1135.13

- India: 349.97 - 490.3

- Indonesia: 198.96 - 256.11

- USA: 223.03 - 243.42

- Brazil: 141.45 - 157.85

Other countries with a high number of social network users include Bangladesh, Mexico, Vietnam, the Philippines, Japan and Russia.

A country's influence on social media companies' growth can be seen in the way India has influenced the social media scene since mid-2020. In June, it banned the Chinese social app TikTok, citing national security and data security concerns, and suddenly the app's growth declined; at the same time, Snapchat was lapped up by people quitting TikTok, and its numbers, which were not growing much before that, rose appreciably.

Social media consumption by nationality

The Philippines is supposed to be on top when it comes to *per capita consumption* of social media. On average, a Filipino spends 4:15 hours a day on social media as against the global average of 2 hours 25 minutes a day.

The average time spent per day on social media by people of other top social media consuming nations is as follows.

- Columbia: 3 hours 49 minutes
- Brazil: 3:42
- Kenya: 3:41
- Nigeria: 3:32
- South Africa: 3:27

Social network penetration in different countries

Countries differ widely in the penetration of social networks in the population. The following data of top and some other selected countries shows the percentage of people in that country using the top social network. The global average is 49%:

- UAE: 99%
- Taiwan: 88
- South Korea: 87
- China: 72
- USA: 70
- India: 29
- Kenya: 17
- Nigeria: 13

SIZES OF MAJOR SOCIAL MEDIA ENTITIES IN TERMS OF USERS/ TRAFFIC

The number of monthly active users on major social media entities in early 2021 were as follows [figures in million].

Please note that there are six social media platforms with more than one billion active monthly users, and three of them with a total of nearly 5.3 billion active monthly users (Facebook, Instagram and WhatsApp) are owned by Facebook.

- Facebook: 2740
- YouTube: 2291
- WhatsApp: 2000
- Facebook Messenger: 1300
- Instagram: 1221
- WeChat: 1213
- TikTok: 689
- QQ: 617
- Douyin: 600
- Sina Weibo: 511
- QZone: 517
- Telegram: 500
- Snapchat: 498
- Kuaishou: 481
- Pinterest: 442
- Reddit: 430
- Twitter: 353
- Quora: 300

KEY DATA OF MAJOR SOCIAL MEDIA ENTITIES

[This data may not be mutually comparable, as different sources have been used, including research companies, data aggregators and websites of social media , and the reference dates are also not the same. It should still serve the purpose of showing the strengths of a platform.]

Facebook

- Facebook is the largest social media platform.

- India, followed by the US, Indonesia, Brazil and Mexico have the largest number of Facebook users.

- Half of its users tend to visit the platform more than once a day and about 23% access it daily in the US.

- In the US, about 52% of all adult consumers use it for getting news, which is more than entertainment or engagement.

- Facebook (company) generated $69 billion in ad revenue in 2020.

- There are more than 10 million Facebook groups.

- About 15% of all content on Facebook is in the form of images and 34.7% in videos.

- On a day, the platform generates videos for 3000 years of watch-time.

YouTube

- YouTube is the second most popular social sharing site and also the second most used search engine.

- People watch 1 billion hours of videos on YouTube every day.

- YouTube generates more than $15 billion ad revenue in a year.

Instagram

- Instagram has the most users in the US, India, Brazil, Indonesia and Russia.

- 70% of its users are up to 34 years of age.

- Top interests on the platform are travel, music, food and drink, fashion, and movies.

- About 60% of Instagram users access the platform at least once a day.

- Most of the content on Instagram is photos (59%), followed by carousels (26%). Video posts constitute 15% of the content.

WhatsApp

- India, followed by Brazil are the biggest users of this instant messaging app.

- WhatsApp comes with many other features including VOIP (=internet voice calls) and money transfer.

- More than 65 billion messages are exchanged on the platform in a day.

Twitter

- The largest number of Twitter users are in the US, Japan, India, Brazil and the UK.

- Males use Twitter more as compared to females.

Snapchat

- Snapchat is most popular in the US, followed by India, France and the UK.

- 61% of Snapchat users are women.

- 82% of Snapchat users are up to 34 years old.

Reddit

- The US has the most Reddit users, followed by the UK and Canada.

- It has more than 50,000 active communities.

- 38% of Reddit users are technology enthusiasts.

LinkedIn

- There are 740 million registered users on LinkedIn in early 2021.

- Most numbers of LinkedIn users are in the US, followed by India, China, Brazil and the UK.

- LinkedIn users tend to be more educated and with higher incomes.

- Unlike other social media apps, slightly less than half of the LinkedIn users (43%) access it on devices other than smartphones.

- More than 40 million firms are listed on the platform.

Pinterest

- US has the biggest number of Pinterest users.

- Females account for 72% of users on Pinterest.

- Most Pinterest users are below 40 years of age. Most pinners (who post on Pinterest) are up to 29 years old.

WeChat

- WeChat is China's superapp, with many functions other than social media, including online shopping and money transfer.

- WeChat is supposed to be censored by China, and many countries have banned or blocked the app on reports of use of its data by Chinese authorities.

Sina Weibo

- This Chinese micro-blogging platform has more than 500 million registered users.

QQ

- QQ is a Chinese instant messaging platform, with an international variant, QQ International.

- It has more than one billion registered users across 80+ countries.

TikTok

- About 60% of TikTok users are below 24 years of age.

- 90% of users access the app at least once a day.

- TikTok was among the most downloaded app in 2019 and 2020 on Apple App Store as well as Google Play Store.

OTHER DATA

Time spent online

People have been consuming content on social media and other online platforms, often sharing one's content with the other. Therefore, it is also interesting to know the overall online content consumption.

The following is the latest global data on how much time people spend on average per day on different types of devices/ platforms:

- Time spent on internet: 6 hrs, 54 minutes
- Time spent on mobile phone: 4:10
- Time spent on social media: 2:25
- Time spent on listening to streaming music: 1:31
- Time spent playing video game on a game console: 1:16
- Time spent on listening to podcasts: 0:54

In a survey conducted by WeAreSocial during COVID-19, people said they will continue with some of the new online activities they had adopted during the pandemic.

- 20% said they would continue watching more shows and films on streaming services
- 16% to spend longer time on messenger services
- 15% to spend longer times on social media
- 14% to listen to more music streaming services
- 10% would spend more time on mobile apps
- 10% would spend more time playing computer/ video games
- 5.5% would create and upload videos
- 4.2% would listen to more podcasts

Lifespan of social media messages

Though the actual lifespan of a post depends on many factors, the following data widely shared on the web captures the sense that social media posts have a small lifespan:

- Tweet: 18 minutes
- Facebook post: 5 hours
- Instagram post: 21 hours
- LinkedIn post: 24 hours
- YouTube video: 20 days
- Pinterest post: 4 months
- Blog post: 2 years

TODAY'S MAJOR SOCIAL MEDIA ENTITIES AND THEIR MAIN FEATURES

If you skipped the previous chapter, I would advise you to go back to appreciate how important the major social media platforms are in terms of their company's size, number of account holders and geographical dominance. In the present chapter, only the most popular platforms have been picked up.

Facebook is, without doubt, the biggest social media entity today. Under its influence, its major competitors such as Myspace and Orkut have faded away and Google Plus had to change its model to somehow remain relevant. In the micro-blogging arena, Twitter is the leader. YouTube is the king of video sharing. In chat, WhatsApp and Facebook Messenger are top contenders. Instagram comes on top as visual-focused socialization entity. LinkedIn happens to be the most popular business social media platform.

Some large social media platforms are China-based and focused mostly on China and Chinese population abroad. These include WeChat, Sina Weibo and QQ. Since they are not cosmopolitan in nature and approach (QQ is now expanding with its international edition, though), I have omitted them in this chapter.

Isn't it interesting that these social media sites have their accounts on other social media platforms, e.g. Facebook has a Twitter account, Instagram a Facebook account and Twitter a Facebook page, and all have a blog!

Note that all social media platforms now have mobile apps, and the features on desktop and mobile versions vary. While some migrated from desktop version to mobile version, some others (e.g. Instagram, WhatsApp) debuted on mobile platforms and later came out with desktop versions too. Please also note that in this fast-changing world of social apps, some features mentioned in this book may have disappeared or changed in look and feel by the time you read it.

Let us look at the main differentiators of these individual platforms.

FACEBOOK

Facebook is a social media platform for all ages and genders. It is also popular across regions. Youth and middle-aged people are its main users but its popularity among young adults and teens seems to be declining. Globally, more women than men use Facebook.

Facebook is available in a large number of languages. Anybody over 13 years of age can open an account on the platform. Once you have opened an account on Facebook, you get to see posts from your friends and others in a stream – this is called your *newsfeed*. You can customize the newsfeed in many ways by going to *settings*. Your own posts and other details are called your *profile* or *timeline*, which can also be customized. There are many privacy features, which can be modified to allow or disallow your personal details and posts to some or all visitors.

Networking on Facebook happens in many ways, for example:

- Making friends and following others.
- Posting on your own and others' pages, timelines, groups, etc.
- Making pages and following others' pages.
- Opening groups and making members, and being member of others' groups.
- Commenting on others' posts and comments.
- Liking and sharing others' content.
- Tagging others on your posts.

Typically, the Facebook *newsfeed* carries posts from others. Though you would expect it to carry posts published by your friends and those you follow, Facebook rather uses an algorithm to decide what should be served to you. It gives importance to promoted (=paid for) content and content that you usually watch (e.g. funny videos, tutorials, posts on sports). In fact, as of 2021, you would see on your newsfeed less of your friends' posts and much more the content decided by Facebook.

There are numerous *groups* on Facebook – some open, some needing approval and some closed. People having common interests can share information, updates and views on groups. You can open your own group and have different settings for the group too. Once you join a group, you see the posts put in by other members of the group.

Facebook allows you to open a *page*. The Facebook page is not a single page but is a collection of articles, like a blog. The page is more serious a place than the timeline. Facebook pages are usually created for branding oneself, an organization or a product. It suits businesses to have their pages on Facebook. Facebook gives detailed analytics, called *insights*, on the performance of the page.

Facebook also has a feature called *stories*. Stories are collections of photos and videos that you would post, for example about a picnic or birthday party, so that your friends and followers can view them all in one go. Stories disappear after 24 hours.

Another interesting feature on Facebook is *memories*. It records events in your life and your interactions with friends. If you put this feature on, Facebook would post a *memory* on your timeline on the day of your birthday, wedding anniversary or starting friendship with someone.

Facebook allows you to *tag* others to your posts. When you tag someone, his profile links to the post or individual photograph where you have tagged that person.

Facebook has a marketplace and its app also has a feature (not in all countries) for money transfer.

A large number of websites and apps use Facebook for signing into them.

Facebook offers advertising on the platform, which people use for promoting their websites, blog posts, products and services, and so on. Since Facebook gets billions of page-views, businesses like to advertise on this platform.

In recent times, Facebook is vigorously promoting the posting of videos. It also has integrated its *Messenger* with the main Facebook account [more on it in <u>WhatsApp and Facebook Messenger</u> section below].

Facebook claims to have taken many steps in recent years against the misuse of the platform for the spread of fake news, child pornography, terrorism, election manipulation, etc. However, it has been embroiled in a number of controversies relating to leakage and deliberate sale of data, and is criticized for not doing enough against the misuse of the platform. The platform is also supposed to be leading to social media addiction and associated physical and mental/ emotional ailments among youth. These have been discussed in detail in chapters dealing specifically with these issues.

TWITTER

Unlike Facebook, Twitter allows posts of a shorter length – of up to 280 characters only. Within that limit, one can post text, links, images and videos. The posts on Twitter are called *tweets*.

Networking on Twitter occurs mainly in the following ways.

- Tweeting, also with links to websites and other web entities.

- Sharing others' content (mainly retweeting).

- Following others.

- Liking others' content.

- Mentioning others in tweets.

- Sending direct messages to one another.

- Making 'lists' of useful accounts.

- Creating 'moments'.

- Hashtagging.

A Twitter account can be opened by anybody of 13 years of age or older. You can also open a Twitter account in the name of your company or a brand.

What you see when you open your Twitter account is the feed of tweets from all the accounts you follow and also tweets chosen by Twitter based on its algorithm and commercial considerations.

Only your tweets are listed in your *profile* or *timeline*. You can *pin* an important tweet on top of your timeline.

Twitter also presents the latest *trends* – listing the expressions that are currently being talked about by a large number of people on Twitter – and you can customize the trends according to your location.

You can *follow* a person and later *unfollow* him; you can also *mute* a person for some time or *block* him forever.

You can create *lists* or groups of important accounts so that if you want to check only their tweets, you can do that in one click. This helps in getting updates from top Twitterati on a particular topic or event. You can make your lists public or private.

An easy way to get information relating to a topic of your choice is to create *moments*. By default, all relevant public tweets on that topic are curated under that moment, but you can also customize it further.

Twitter uses some symbols for special purposes. @ is used to *mention* an account (e.g. *@barackobama* denotes US ex-President Barack Obama's Twitter account). # (=hashtag) is used for tagging a tweet with some event, place, person, issue, etc.

Hashtagging or use of # is a major activity on Twitter. You attach the # symbol before an expression to state that you tag the tweet with that expression. For example, if you put *#blogging* anywhere inside a tweet, the tweet carries this hashtag. Now if anybody searches for blogging, this tweet is served in his search results. During major sporting events, mishaps, annual days and elections, people put already popular hashtags on their tweets and thus that hashtag becomes more and more popular and starts *trending*.

Hashtags serve many purposes. People keep using hashtags to show alignment with a topic. Companies use hashtags for their new products. Political leaders use them to widen their fan-base. Activists use them for gathering support for the cause. Hashtags are also used to have a *Twitter chat* on a topic.

The medium suits the dissemination of all forms of messages in real-time. As compared to Facebook where most people are both givers and receivers of information, the majority of account holders on Twitter use it for hearing from/ about others and therefore they depend upon it for getting alerts and updates. This becomes an easy way for fans to track celebrities, and therefore Twitter suits public figures of all types.

Twitter is also used by news-sources to keep giving real-time breaking news and updates, and thus has become a popular source of news.

Because tweets get distributed instantaneously to all the followers, Twitter has found special use in times of natural calamities – before, during and after - for alerting, giving the latest information and messages, and coordinating relief operations.

The instant nature of Twitter also helps brands in the resolution of complaints.

When you are highly popular on Twitter, you are given the tag of a *social influencer*. Influencers earn big sums for endorsing brands. There also are reports that on one hand, the follower-count on Twitter is sometimes bloated artificially and on the other, influencers are indiscreet in promoting brands. This topic has been discussed as a separate section in Social Media Beyond Personal Socialization chapter.

INSTAGRAM

Younger than Facebook and Twitter, Instagram is the visual-focused social networking platform of today. Instagram has gathered a massive user base and has left other visual-focused social media platforms (e.g. Pinterest, Snapchat) far behind. By allowing instant socialization in addition to sharing of pictures, it has also gone far ahead of photo-sharing sites such as Flickr in terms of social engagement.

Initially started as a mobile app for instant sharing of pictures taken from mobile phones (hence the name *'insta'*) with one's friends, Instagram now has features much beyond that. In addition to images and videos, the platform now allows streaming of videos of up to one-hour duration. Its feature called *IGTV* or vertical videos is also popular among users because such videos can be captured by and watched on a mobile phone without the need to tilt the device.

On opening the Instagram app, you see the latest posts from the ones you follow, and like on Facebook newsfeed, you are served trending content and that chosen by the Instagram algorithm based on your browsing habits and the platform's commercial intent.

The main social networking and sharing activities on this platform are:

- Publishing posts, which mostly are photographs and videos, with or without short captions.

- Creating stories with images and videos.

- Following others and being followed by others.

- Liking others' posts with emojis, and sharing others' posts.

- Commenting on others' posts.

- Hashtagging.

Instagram is highly youth-centric, and the majority of its users are women. The rate of engagement on Instagram is found to be higher than that on Facebook and Twitter. Being primarily a visual medium, it is lapped up by individuals and brands dealing with beauty, fashion, lifestyle, celebrities, décor, cooking, photography, travel and culture.

Like Twitter, established Instagram accounts get a large number of followers. These *influencers* can then monetize their status by posting sponsored content, recommending products, making favorable comments, and so on.

After Facebook acquired Instagram in 2012, the two apps have seen some integration though both maintain separate identities. You can log into your Instagram account with Facebook profile and follow your Facebook friends on Instagram directly through Instagram app.

YOUTUBE

With the availability of higher bandwidth, better cameras, smartphones with better specs and powerful apps, video has become the medium in which more and more content sharing and socialization is taking place on social media apps. It has been predicted that about 76% of mobile bandwidth will be consumed on video transmission by 2025.

All major social media platforms utilize the features of smartphones to publish and share videos. Yet, YouTube rules the video world. It is interesting that YouTube also is the second most popular search engine after Google!

Started as a video sharing platform, YouTube mostly remains so. It is not as 'social' as Instagram and other similar social media platforms as it is not used primarily for networking or instant exchange of short videos. Socialization happens because the platform allows the users to keep posting videos, opening their *channels* and even live streaming with almost no limit. People comment on others' videos, subscribe to them and share them on their playlists on YouTube or in other places (e.g. on their blogs).

The platform pays to video creators based on the popularity of individual videos and therefore a very large number of people run their channels with tutorials and funny/ exciting videos. Many new platforms, usually with a localized appeal, have come up on the same model and have become popular among the younger population.

What you see when you log in to your YouTube account on desktop or app is trending videos, updates from the channels you have subscribed and videos according to your browsing habits. YouTube inserts advertisements in videos when they play.

YouTube has, besides its main app, apps on gaming, music, kids, etc.

LINKEDIN

LinkedIn has been the world's topmost business-focused social network since its inception and retains the top slot in this niche. A large number of businesses maintain their accounts on LinkedIn. Aspirants as well as established names in various professional fields and employment levels use the platform for improving their brand value or for sourcing talent.

LinkedIn has a variety of features for social interaction and networking. The major ways in which people use this platform are:

- Inviting people to connect, and joining others' networks.
- Following others.
- Commenting on others' posts.
- Validating others' skills and specializations.
- Recommending people for jobs and assignments.
- Making and joining groups.
- Writing articles and commenting on others' articles.
- Giving and getting employment advice.

Since LinkedIn is used for showcasing one's professional assets, and one's profile gets validation from others, employers often consider potential employees' LinkedIn profiles for managerial and professional jobs.

To add professionalism to the platform, LinkedIn allows users to create *articles*, which are like blog posts. Others can comment on these posts and *like* them.

When you log in to your LinkedIn account, you get to see notifications, messages and articles based mostly on your profile and those you follow. If you are an expert or a high-ranking professional/ manager, you likely get a stream of messages from prospective employees and assignment-seekers.

WHATSAPP AND FACEBOOK MESSENGER

The omnipresence of smartphones and the availability of wireless internet in most parts of the globe has resulted in all-time connectivity. Instant messaging apps exploit this for real-time communication, content-sharing and socialization. Though the old SMS is still useful when there is no internet connection, and for phone-based identification and security checks, etc., the versatility of instant messaging and chatting apps leaves

SMS far behind as a medium of communication. These apps suit not only personal but also business and crisis communication (messaging at the time of calamities, etc.).

On these apps, you can communicate with other account holders one-to-one and send them pictures, videos and other types of files/ data. What makes them 'social' is that the messages from your friends and your responses stream to and fro in real-time. In addition, the provision to have *groups,* and communicate and share documents or media securely and privately within the group, make them eminently suitable for community building.

These apps are primarily for use on smartphones but have their desktop avatars too. Because of their instant nature, and light and secure architecture, they have been introducing non-chat features e.g. audio and video calling, group calling, file transfer and online monetary transactions.

WhatsApp is the most used chatting app and another app from the same Facebook family, Facebook Messenger, gives it competition. Facebook Messenger app automatically integrates with Facebook app. Unlike other platforms, on which 13 years is the minimum age for having an account, one needs to be 16 years old to have an account on WhatsApp. WhatsApp has also introduced disappearing messages, a bigger capacity of group video calls, and more e-commerce features.

OTHER SOCIAL MEDIA PLATFORMS

There are many hundred social media platforms present in early 2021. Some of them are big enough to give competition to the top platforms, e.g. Snapchat, Pinterest and Telegram. However, the smaller ones focus on small audiences with special needs (e.g. language) to carve out a niche for themselves. Sometimes, instead of competing with others, they allow for seamless sharing of content on other platforms, some cater to special communities, some to enterprises only. Dozens of these take birth every month but many of them die an early death.

Google Plus [https://plus.google.com/discover] needs a special mention here. This platform started in 2011 with some well-imagined features and was buzzing with activity till around 2015-16, but could not stand ground against Facebook despite some re-designs. Google finally closed down the app in 2019 for common users and launched an enterprise-level social app, ***Google Currents***.

Myspace [https://myspace.com] ruled the social networking scene between 2005 and 2009 and was especially popular among young people. At one stage, it even wanted to acquire Facebook but soon succumbed to Facebook's popularity. The platform still has millions of profiles but is now focused mostly on sharing music and videos, and lacks apps on Google's Play Store and Apple's App Store.

Myspace suffered badly when a major data breach occurred in 2016 in which personal data of millions of its account holders was circulated on the dark web.

Pinterest [https://pinterest.com] was launched in 2009 and became a popular social bookmarking and sharing site on visually appealing subjects. The platform, though surpassed by a huge margin by Instagram, is still popular. It allows users to *'pin'* (=bookmark and paste) appealing photographs and videos to their boards. This feature of simultaneously bookmarking and sharing images/ videos makes it especially suitable for people (especially girls) to share their photos as well as images of their creations (e.g. recipes, wardrobe) and visually appealing activities (e.g. travel, social functions, dance). Pinterest's business pages are harnessed well by retailers of visually rich products. Pinterest now allows and monetization.

On your Pinterest home page, you get a stream of pictures in areas of your liking/ choosing. When you follow others, your feed gets visuals recently uploaded by them on their *pinboard* or business page.

Snapchat [https://www.snapchat.com] came in 2011 with a host of features such as the use of mobile phone for taking a picture, posting it instantly and it being there only for a short duration. More features such as the use of short videos and putting funny effects on the photo/ video on the *'snaps'* (=short-life visual messages) have made it a very vibrant medium of self-expression.

The short duration of availability of visual content has led to millions of fans swearing by the platform, as it focuses on instant sharing of one's status and emotions that need not be kept for long. Of late, the platform has allowed saving the content so that the fleeting content, if of permanent value, can be retained.

Snapchat too lost to Instagram by a big margin but has got a boost in 2020.

TikTok (initially Douyin, launched in China) [https://www.tiktok.com] is a popular app for sharing short videos. It came into being in 2016. It merged with musical.ly in 2018, and the combined community of users now spans across the globe. The majority of its users are youngsters who love to experiment with their mobile phone cameras. The video-sharing app has been mired in controversies over its use by Chinese authorities for data collection and snooping, and has faced blocking or ban in some countries. Under criticism for allowing all types of content (that was said to be one of the reasons for its popularity among teens and young adults), it started labeling false or misleading content in 2021.

Telegram [https://telegram.org] is an instant messaging app with many features. It is gaining popularity because of its focus on secure communication. Unlike WhatsApp where groups can accommodate only a few hundred members, Telegram groups can have 2,00,000 members. One can have the app open simultaneously on more than one device.

BLOGGING

You would agree that blogging is a special segment of social media and therefore needs a separate chapter. If you are interested in even more details on different aspects (for example, technical, social and legal) of blogging, *The Manual of Blogging* [ref 55] is the resource I would refer you to.

Blogging has undergone an enormous transformation over the years. The initial blogs that came up during the mid-1990s were in the form of simple HTML pages that were used by web technologists for jotting down updates in their field. The advent of blogging platforms (LiveJournal, Blogger) metamorphosed blogging into a mainstream web activity as now making a blog became simple and it did not need any knowledge of web technologies.

Blogging gave everybody a wonderful tool to express themselves and broadcast their views without the need for a publisher or broadcaster. The ability to comment and share blog posts allowed bloggers to socialize online.

Since then, many new platforms have emerged, mostly providing the blogging tools free of cost. New features such as posting images, grouping posts, their seamless display, and commenting were added, followed by even more advanced features such as styling, posting videos and e-commerce facilities.

2005-06 saw the peak of blogging. It presented such great possibility of information sharing that it was being predicted in those years that blogs would soon overtake print and electronic media and might even make them redundant.

Then came the social networking and instant messaging platforms, and blogging took the back seat as a medium of socialization. Nevertheless, as a medium for publishing long-form content, blogs have maintained their relevance.

BLOGGING TODAY

The terms *blog* and *blogging* have acquired broader meanings over time. The initial blogs were web diaries. In fact, the word *'blog'* happens to come from *web* and *log* (=diary).

Blog can be defined in different ways and, after researching on the subject of blogging, I have adopted the following definition of blogging as it encompasses all types of blogs as of today:

Publishing of long-form content on the web on a regular basis.

A blog, by that definition, would be:

A website published on the web, whose main content is in the form of posts that are updated regularly.

Please note that the initial narrow definitions of 'blogging' and 'blog' can no longer accommodate what is today understood by these terms. When blogging was the main social media activity, 'blog' referred to a standalone website – either an independent domain [e.g. www.example.com] or part of the main domain of the blogging platform in which it was located [e.g. www.example.blogspot.com]. But when social networking platforms started dominating, people started using 'blogging' and 'blog' to include all social activity on the web. So, people today say, they blog on Instagram or Twitter or Facebook when they actively publish posts on these platforms. Podcasting and publishing video posts on YouTube or TikTok are also non-traditional forms of blogging.

If 'blogging' is reserved for long-form content to differentiate it from short-form/ instant/ transitional content on social networking platforms, some of these sites have come up with blogging. For example, one can open *pages* on Facebook and LinkedIn, which are suitable for posting long-form content of long-lasting value.

Blogging has also graduated from just sharing of personal information to publishing for professional purposes. In its early days, most blogging was for sharing personal information and views but later, people were attracted towards it as a means to earn online and to showcase their professional talent. Online advertising through AdWords, AdSense and affiliate networks grew and many bloggers during heydays of blogging made handsome money. Though thousands of bloggers still maintain their blogs for personal blogging or as a hobby, the trend is towards harnessing the potential of serious, long-form content for professional purposes (including blogging for science communication and edublogging) and making money.

HOW ARE BLOGS OPENED AND MAINTAINED?

Let us start with the technical nature of a typical blog. A blog is nothing but a website in which there are many articles (called *posts*) that are written over time and are displayed one after the other. The usual arrangement of posts is reverse-chronological, i.e., the latest ones come on top while the previous ones are pushed down. Individual posts, and the blog itself, have separate *URLs* or web addresses. You can put text, images and media on these posts and can allow visitors to comment on and share the posts. You can also create standalone web pages, often called *pages* to differentiate them from *posts*, which do not go down in the stack when new pages/ posts are published.

For the blog to be available on the World Wide Web, there are two essential requirements: one, that the blog must have a unique identity or *domain name* and two, the content must be *hosted* on a server that is connected through internet. To meet the first requirement, the domain name of the blog (or any other website) must be registered with a domain name registrar and it must be kept alive year after year. For keeping the content available to visitors, the website/ blog must be hosted with a web hosting company and the hosting too must be renewed again and again.

When you open your blog with a *free* blogging platform, you need not bother about domain name registration or web hosting because both are taken care of by the platform. Your blog, however, gets the domain name that looks subordinate to the main domain [e.g. *example.wordpress.com* is a sub-domain of *wordpress.com*]. You also have to abide by the policies of the platform. If you opt to design your blog yourself, and pay for domain name registration and web hosting, you are free to give it the domain name of your liking [e.g. *example.com* or *example.info* or *example.uk*] and put whatever content you like on the blog. Such blogs are called *self-hosted* blogs.

A number of software suites are available online, which can create self-hosted blogs without much knowledge or underlying technologies. These are called *content management systems* (CMSs) and website builders.

The majority of blogs run on free blogging platforms. *Blogger* and *Wordpress* are the two main free blogging platforms, followed by *Tumblr*, *LiveJournal* and *Medium*. There are many other free and paid blogging platforms. Of the platforms named here, *Blogger* and *Wordpress* allow the maximum customization while *Medium* and *LiveJournal* allow the least.

New types of social media, e.g. social networking, differ from blogging in being more instant and 'short-form' and therefore there is much more engagement on their platforms. Instant messaging apps make the engagement even faster. This has led to reduced direct engagement on blogs. Yet, if used properly, the engagement on social networking and chat platforms can be made to complement engagement with the blog's target audience. Bloggers take several measures to achieve this complementarity. Some important ones are as follows:

- The simplest way is to have cross-links from one platform to the other. A prominent display of such links can be achieved through buttons.

- Modern web technologies allow automatic posting of content from one platform to another but it needs to be done with discretion, for at least two reasons: (i) 'duplicate content' (i.e. same content copy-pasted in different places) is not liked by visitors and search engines alike; and (ii) the same content may not suit different platforms unless the content is manually shaped to suit a particular platform.

- The blog can display feed from the blogger's own social networking platforms (e.g. Twitter) to show the discussion on the blog's topics on those platforms.

- The blog can also have a *widget* showing updates on networked blogs in a community platform so that visitors are encouraged to visit the community through the blog.

- Individual blog posts can have links for direct sharing of individual posts on social networks and bookmarking platforms.

- New posts can be *'pinged'* to many directories and social sites through pinging websites (e.g. http://pingomatic.com).

- New posts can also be submitted on bookmarking and aggregating sites where these are voted, commented upon and shared with others.

Despite the low attention-span of web surfers or the instant and easy nature of social networking, publishing long-form content on the web will likely remain an important activity in all its avatars, i.e. on websites, in the form of news and features, for professional purposes and for expressing oneself. It might also happen that more and more people start getting tired of superfluous and purpose-less engagement on social networks and look for more serious content. I have come across one expert observation [ref 73], which echoes this fact based on ground reality: "...across platforms, things are changing. Audiences are now willing to invest more time and attention in stories they deem to have a higher value." It is also reported that in influencer marketing, brands are now giving less value to just 'likes' or follower count than useful engagement. Medium is the shining example of a successful blogging platform whose reputation and consumer-loyalty rests on readable long-form content.

KEY FEATURES OF FREE BLOGGING PLATFORMS

Free blogs can be opened by registering oneself with any free blogging platform. Usually, there is a *dashboard* that lists all the blogs opened with the same registration. Each blog on the platform has a dashboard of its own, which contains different options, e.g. creation and editing of posts, theme or design customization, layout settings, privacy and engagement settings, and so on. Each of these options has several features depending upon the platform.

Let us talk about key features of the prominent free platforms.

Blogger [https://www.blogger.com]

This is among the earliest blogging platforms and is completely free. On Blogger, blogs can be created just by opening an account and a few clicks afterward. If you already have a Google account (e.g. Gmail, Google Photos or Drive), you can use the same for Blogger also. You have a large number of tools available for customizing the blog. The platform even allows editing of the core code of the underlying *theme* (=design template). Using *gadgets* (=*widgets*), you can add a number of additional features. You can monetize your blog by placing advertisements on it.

A blog created on Blogger has *.blogspot.com* suffix in its domain name. However, the blog's domain name can be changed to an independent domain name (i.e. without *blogspot*) free of cost, by mapping the *blogspot* name to an independent domain name.

Wordpress [https://wordpress.com]

This platform has two variants: (i) *wordpress.org* – a free content management system (CMS), and (ii) *wordpress.com* – a free blogging platform.

Wordpress blogging platform [https://wordpress.com] is similar to Blogger, and blogs created on it have *.wordpress.com* suffix in their domain name. Features like putting third-party codes and advertisements are not available in the free plan. However, one can upgrade the plan, on payment, to get many additional features. Mapping the free blog to an independent domain name (without *wordpress.com* suffix) is also allowed but on payment.

LiveJournal [https://www.livejournal.com]

This free blogging platform does not allow much customization but promotes community building through grouping and commenting.

One can open a blog (called *journal*) free and participate in communities. Some extra frills are available on upgrading the account on payment. No monetization is possible on LiveJournal.

Tumblr [https://www.tumblr.com]

This also is a free platform, with scope for customization through HTML. On payment, it allows custom domains and premium themes. It promotes sharing of content, even anonymously, within the community of Tumblr bloggers. *Re-blogging* or using content from somebody's blog on one's own blog is an allowed activity.

This platform is popular among teens and college-goers, with about half of its bloggers being under 25 years of age. Tumblr had come under criticism for promoting anonymous blogging and being lax on the use of pornography, and in 2018, cleaned itself of much of adult content.

Medium [https://medium.com]

This free blogging platform does not allow customization as of now. With a plain and unobtrusive design, it aims to promote reading of quality content. On payment, one can upgrade the account to a membership account that has some additional features for sharing, reading, etc.

Postach.io [https://postach.io/site]

This blog creation tool works with *Evernote* [https://evernote.com] and turns notes into blog posts. It excels in collaboration and seamlessly makes use of the content curation capability of Evernote.

Other blogging platforms

There are a number of popular blogging platforms that provide blogging services on payment. Such platforms especially suit persons and organizations that would like exclusive features, expandability, maintaining the blog as part of a portal, and personalized customer support. The popular paid blogging platforms are:

- Typepad [http://www.typepad.com],

- Svbtle [https://svbtle.com] and

- Ghost [https://ghost.org]. Ghost can, as a CMS, create blogs for free, but its blogging platform is a paid service.

WEBSITE BUILDERS

While the websites/ platforms mentioned above are more suited for blogging, one can use them for creating standard websites too. A majority of non-blog websites being created today use *Wordpress.org* CMS (more on it in the CMS section below). Conversely, there are many website builders, used primarily for creating non-blog websites, which can be used for creating blogs too.

Some of the available website builders have features beyond blogging platforms. A few have very easy drag-and-drop, template-based and query-based interfaces for easy creation of websites and blogs.

Since website builders are not primarily for creation of blogs, let us just mention some popular names and move ahead:

- Google Sites [https://sites.google.com]

- MovableType [https://www.movabletype.org]

- SquareSpace [https://www.squarespace.com]

- Weebly [https://www.weebly.com]

- Wix [https://www.wix.com]

CONTENT MANAGEMENT SYSTEM (CMS)

CMS is the code that helps users to create digital content (website, blog, application, etc.) and customize its looks and functions through a user-friendly interface. The blogging platforms and website builders mentioned above are in fact different types of CMSs.

Let us talk about three major stand-alone CMSs that run the majority of websites and self-hosted blogs today. These CMSs are highly professional software suites and have almost unlimited functionality and customization options. Unlike free blogging platforms, they do not provide free hosting space or domain name; therefore, after creating the blog, the blogger has to register its domain name and then host it on a web host.

- Wordpress [https://wordpress.org] is the most popular CMS for bloggers wanting to have a self-hosted blog. Over 30 percent of all websites (including blogs) are now created using Wordpress CMS.

- Joomla [https://www.joomla.org] – like Wordpress, it is an all-purpose CMS for creating websites (including blogs). It is considered slightly more difficult for people not familiar with web technologies.

- Drupal [https://www.drupal.org] – Similar to Wordpress and Joomla, it is also a feature-rich CMS.

EARNING FROM BLOGGING

As said earlier, people now get attracted to blogging for earning money more than for socialization.

Bloggers use different ways for monetizing their blogs, e.g.

- By allowing one or more types of advertisements on the blog. With the most common type of advertisements, called *pay per click* (PPC) advertisements, the blogger gets a small sum when a visitor clicks on the advertisement. Google has created *AdSense*, which is the biggest PPC ad-network in the world and is popular among bloggers. Advertisements can also be sourced from *affiliate marketing* companies [e.g. CJ, Shopify, and Clickbank]. These companies aggregate advertisements from many brands and place them on blogs (and other websites) and pay the blogger when someone buys the product through the blog. Some online marketers [e.g. Amazon] directly offer affiliation. Established bloggers can get advertisements from brands directly too.

- By selling others' products through recommendations and reviews. When you give a positive review of a product or service on your blog or recommend it to your visitors, the producer seller or service provider pays you for that. Many bloggers, especially in beauty, fashion and travel niches make good money referring their visitors to companies selling beauty and fashion products, travel packages, hotels, etc. Bloggers in these niches get invitations to press meets, blogger meets and sponsored tours, and thus earn by creating content for promoting businesses. This can extend to paid and sponsored posts, offering discounts through an arrangement with brands, etc.

- By selling one's own products and services. A large number of authors maintain blogs, often giving excerpts of their published books and offering other insights about books, discussing literary matters and giving information about upcoming books. Many bloggers offer online courses, ebooks, etc. relating to their specialization. Some bloggers start their merchandise or services after getting popular, e.g. fashion line, recipes and travel packages. Established bloggers are also seen offering webinars, speaking assignments and endorsements.

- Using the blog as a funnel for getting traffic to the main site. A large number of companies that maintain portals have a blog section, and they use it for introducing new products, giving special previews to loyal visitors, discussing technology and for customer service. It is proven that when blogging is done professionally on corporate portals, it generates loyalty, gets more traffic to the main site, provides valuable feedback and gives new ideas for future products.

- Making blogs and selling them. This is not very common but some bloggers create blogs, maintain them for some time and then sell them.

TECHNOLOGICAL ASPECTS RELATED TO SOCIAL MEDIA

As you would know, most of the content on the World Wide Web is on websites. Websites in turn consist of web pages that carry some code written primarily through a web language called *HTML*. There is a set of rules, called hypertext transfer protocol (HTTP), that allows these pages to be accessed by web browsers (e.g. Internet Explorer, Edge, Firefox, Safari, Chrome, DuckDuckGo). Behind the HTML pages are resources (text, pictures, videos, scripts, code) in the website; web browsers interpret these and present them to the viewer in a human-friendly display.

As new web technologies are emerging, there is a lot of code/ script that is written on the web pages to give the pages a sophisticated look and for varied functionalities that we see on websites today (e.g. login, display options, automatic zooming of pages depending upon the device size, auto-scrolling of pages, feeds and updates from other sites, animations, instant calculations, monetary transactions, and so on).

HTML itself has evolved into *HTML5*, which can add many more features on websites, web apps, etc. than its earlier versions.

Cascading Style Sheets or CSS is another common language on webpages, mostly used for styling their look and feel.

Blogs are nothing but websites, with features for display of new posts, post categorization, commenting, placement of advertisements, etc. They use one or more languages in addition to HTML for enhancing their appeal and functionalities.

Blogger uses *JavaScript*, a scripting language, for adding widgets, etc. Wordpress uses *PHP*, and some of its coding has migrated to JavaScript. JavaScript and related languages are used for adding interactive features on all types of blogs.

Among social networking, social sharing and chat sites, JavaScript is the most popular front-end script (i.e. carries out actions at the user-end) because of its quality to perform functions at the display end itself and to allow interactivity. *Python*, *Java* and *PHP* are the commonly used server-end languages (i.e. they carry out functions while sitting in the server where the platform or website is located).

A mind-boggling array of web/ computer languages has emerged in recent times, each new one with new features that can be exploited on the web. That makes it possible to develop new social media platforms with new ways of serving content, engagement and sharing.

On smartphones, users do not generally go to the desktop versions of social networking and instant messaging sites but use *apps*. Mobile apps are stand-alone programs written in a mix of modern computer languages. They have an advantage over websites in that they are more customizable and fast, can carry out many functions without internet connection, and can seamlessly use camera, microphone and other accessories available on the mobile phone.

I am giving here a glimpse of the number of modern languages used in creating and running modern social media platforms. The list of languages named here is far from exhaustive.

- Facebook uses PHP, Hack, Python, Erlang, C++, XHP, Haskell and JavaScript.

- Twitter uses Scala and Ruby in association with Java, etc.

- Wikipedia uses PHP, Hack and JavaScript.

- Apps for Android smartphones are written in Java (not the same as JavaScript). Apps for Apple phones are created using Swift and Objective C languages.

- WhatsApp and other instant messaging and chat apps are written in languages that allow threading and large-scale real-time message handling, so they use a set of languages including Erlang, FreeBSD and XMPP for back-end functionalities, in addition to the app-making languages mentioned above.

- At the back-end, all platforms have to keep enormous data in servers that have huge storage capacity. They use one of the top database languages (e.g. MySQL, PostgreSQL, and Oracle).

If one of the factors behind the fast groundswell in the usage of social media is the technology behind them, one other equally important factor is that the users do not have to bother about the technology at all. Once the users are served a new functionality, they look for more; the constant demand for more features leads to fast development of new variants of old web/ computer languages or origin of totally new ones. The cycle moves on and on.

Many ancillary technologies have evolved and are available to users. There are many tools, free or paid, for automatic posting from one account to the other (e.g. from blog to Twitter), scheduling posts, following and unfollowing people and other actions that would be difficult to perform manually one by one.

There also are analytical and performance measuring tools. They tell which of your posts perform better, what is the best time to post, what type of audiences respond to your messages, what actions are required for optimizing your account/ blog for search engines, and so on. Twitter itself has a good analytics tool available for users and it runs *Tweetdeck* [https://tweetdeck.twitter.com], a scheduling software.

Search engine optimization of blogs also becomes easy with SEO tools. Many marketing-related tech tools have also come into the market for seamlessly carrying out many marketing functions on websites and social media.

Since technology is neutral regarding how it is used, some of it is abused and misused for unethical and criminal purposes. Some tools automatically send spam and harmful backlinks, post wrong messages on behalf of others, steal data, hack accounts. The tools for automation, scheduling, SEO, etc. are also prone to reckless use, which may not be criminal but distorts the working of social media.

At the higher end of tech spectrum, there are tools that can analyze millions of engagements in real-time and then intervene. Even super-computers are used for analyzing data. Such tools are generally available to technology companies and government agencies. Such tools are also reported to be in use by criminal syndicates, state actors (government agencies that work to hurt other governments) and rogue organizations.

An important fact relating to the present-day social media platforms that is often lost sight of is that though social media looks highly democratized and distributed, it is totally under the control of a few. You can have instant communication on WhatsApp only because all your data lies in WhatsApp's servers, and you are served others' data through its extremely powerful software and according to what its algorithms decide. The user feels that *he* controls *his* Facebook account behind a password, but the reality is that his account (or what he sees on his smartphone) is just the client-end display! We would discuss in other chapters how this control on data results in issues relating to privacy, safety and security of account holders.

If you are interested in a discussion on what might lie in the future in the field of technology, you may like to visit the last section of <u>The History of Social Media</u> chapter.

SOCIAL MEDIA BEYOND PERSONAL SOCIALIZATION

In this chapter, let us discuss how social media is being used for moneymaking: business, brand building, marketing, social influence, monetization, etc. We would also discuss social media use in other fields such as politics and elections, social work and education.

Let us appreciate that social media is being used in almost all areas of human activity, and it is not possible to list them all. A few important areas and examples should suffice to show the range of activities that this wonderful medium of communication is contributing to.

It is interesting to note that many information and communication technologies have taken birth to meet personal needs and have been adopted for professional and business/ commercial purposes. For example, SMS came as a quick alternative to phone calls and acted as a medium of socialization too for some time, but it is now used mostly for verification purposes for opening accounts and monetary transactions. Blogging started with the intent of sharing technical information among the peer, then bloomed as a means of self-expression and social networking. A good number of new bloggers of today use their blogs for promoting a brand or making money – and not for personal socialization. Major social sharing, networking and chat sites of today – Facebook, Instagram, Twitter, WhatsApp, YouTube – are still used mainly for personal socialization but are being used more and more for non-personal purposes.

Some ways social media is being used beyond personal communication are:

- Use of instant messaging apps for official and business communication. WhatsApp and Telegram – especially their 'group' features – are widely used for such communication.

- Use of social media (mainly Twitter) by celebrities, politicians, etc. for brand building. Public figures in visual professions (cinema, modeling, dance) are active on Instagram, Snapchat and Pinterest.

Established thought leaders in different fields often maintain a blog.

- Use of social media in elections. Political parties and politicians use (and abuse) social media for spreading positive messages about themselves and deriding their adversaries.

- Use of social media for money-making and promoting business.

- Use of specialized platforms. LinkedIn is used for employment-related networking. Educational blogs are used for teaching purposes. Forums and Q-A sites are used for information sharing and seeking answers in specific areas.

- Webinars are used by a large number of organizations and governments for discussion as well as putting their points of view on serious subjects.

- Not-for-profit, charity and activist organizations use social media for creating awareness and seeking donations.

- Governments use social media for connecting with citizens, providing them public services and redressing their grievances.

- Government agencies also use social media for tracking illegal and anti-social activities.

- Social media is used during calamities and man-made disasters for communication and delivery of services.

Social media is also used for criminal purposes. This has been discussed in detail in <u>Social Media and Crime</u> chapter. Its use (read misuse) by official and other agencies, political parties and other actors for creating and spreading misinformation is one big area of concern. This has been discussed in <u>Misinformation and Fake news</u> section of <u>Social Media as Mass Media and Medium of Free Expression</u> chapter.

Let us discuss in detail the use of social media in key areas.

USE OF SOCIAL MEDIA FOR BUSINESS, EARNING

Social media is used by almost all businesses - big and small — one way or the other, and for different purposes. Individuals interested in earning online also make good use of social media for making money directly or using it to bolster their other streams of earning.

Let us look at some common ways business takes place on/ through/ supported by social media:

- Use of social media by individuals for selling products and services. Authors use them, especially blogs, for selling their books. Some sell tutorials, some ebooks. Bloggers use their blogs to sell all types of merchandise and services. Blog often is made the fulcrum and landing page for display and sale of products or services while other social media entities are used for pulling people to the blog. Instagram and Pinterest are extensively used for visually-appealing products.

- Blogging sometimes gives rise to entrepreneurship. Many bloggers (having standard blogs or blogs on YouTube/ Instagram) in travel, photography, cooking, beauty and fashion niches have opened up their stores or agencies after getting established as bloggers.

- Content on blogs in itself can be a great commodity for earning through it. Blogs are monetized in different ways (mostly by placing advertisements) out of the traffic and goodwill generated primarily due to content. Blog monetization has been covered also in <u>Blogging</u> chapter, and so I will not dwell on this here any further.

- Other platforms also come in handy to sell one's content. Photographs and other forms of images are sold through photo-sharing sites such as Flickr. YouTube and a number of video-sharing platforms/ apps are used for creating video content and monetizing traffic.

- Businesses use social networking platforms for sharing information and getting feedback. Blogs and Facebook pages are in wide use for this purpose. Twitter is often used by consumers to air their grievances, and savvy companies turn these into goodwill by promptly looking into the issues faced by people.

- Big companies have blogs as part of their portals for drawing quality traffic and goodwill to the main site, and improving website SEO.

- Social media helps to connect with customers. Since most customers use social media for personal and professional purposes, it helps businesses to be on social media. That includes direct communication as well as advertisements.

- Social media is used not only to serve existing customers but also for reaching out to potential customers. All major social networking and instant messaging platforms are used by brands for promotion and advertising, especially during seasonal sales, new launches, etc.

- Use of social networking platforms by businesses for brand building has attained significance. Main platforms used for this purpose are Facebook, Twitter and Instagram. Some companies are also reported to be using social platforms for generating negative publicity for their competitors.

- In business circles, 'enterprise social networking' or ESN is finding more and more acceptance. It refers to social networking within big firms, and encompasses existing channels of communication (e.g. intranet) and focuses on the use of online social networks or social relations among people who share business interests and/or activities.

- Social media platforms are now themselves generating enormous money out of advertisements, providing premium services and sharing consumer data.

How social media helps businesses

Let us devote some time to the rationale behind the significantly high potential of earning from social media and actual use scenarios relating to business.

One. Better communication. It is expected that customers are more receptive to business messages conveyed through social media because organic social media communication is more credible as compared to that through emails, press releases and advertisements.

In addition, social media is not a passive one-way medium of communication, unlike traditional media. Interactions and user-generated content (comments, shares, likes, etc.) multiply the impact of the original content, sometimes many times over.

Social media is a highly potent source of feedback, which can be used for improving products, getting ideas for future innovation, changing marketing strategies, etc. Social media-savvy firms make good use of 'social listening' or monitoring and analyzing conversations on social media and acting on them.

Two. Branding and thought leadership. When businesses communicate through social media channels, they are seen to be proactive and friendly (of course, only if they communicate in the right way).

Social media helps in brand building and brand recall. Since a large segment of the population spends more time on social media than on newspapers, magazines and television put together, it makes sense to be active on social media more than on traditional media.

Social media helps greatly in fighting negativity and competition. Social media is perhaps the best way to fight misinformation that might spread due to some product defect or other reason.

As buyers give importance to reviews and comments on blogs, apps and social networks, it helps greatly to have a positive image on social media. A great number of empirical studies have found that buying decisions, especially of the younger generation, get influenced by comments on social media.

Three. Low costs, better results. Advertisement rates are lower on social media platforms as compared to the mainstream media (print and electronic media, outdoor media). Besides, ads can be repeated, varied and customized to meet the requirements of different platforms, thus allowing one to dovetail messages according to the media.

On social media, it is easy to target messages to a specific gender, age group, social segment or region. In addition, most social media platforms make use of user data to serve promotional content to suit individual user's interests. Social media, thus, is highly cost-efficient and generates a higher return on investment (RoI).

Social media is online and can lead to instant returns. If people like your content or are convinced by your sales pitch, they are likely to instantly take a buying decision.

Four. Customer relations. When used properly, social media can improve customer relations and help in solving customers' problems. Twitter is a great platform for this purpose. Other platforms and blogs also have features that suit businesses.

As mentioned earlier, companies that care for social media feedback use such feedback to their advantage.

Unfortunately, most firms and other organizations (especially government-run service providers) tend to use social media half-heartedly – just creating profiles, not regularly updating, having poorly written content, and casually responding to visitors' comments or complaints. Such an approach towards consumers can hurt worse on social media than elsewhere because social media has raised consumer expectations and it amplifies negative comments.

Five. Empirical proof. The points discussed above are not merely theoretical concepts. Studies have shown that proper use of social media actually helps businesses. Let me share a few examples.

Sproutsocial [https://sproutsocial.com] reports some interesting findings based on its study on use of social media by small businesses. [ref 65]:

- There is 57.5 percent likelihood of people buying from a brand that they follow on social media.

- 71% people are more likely to buy after a positive social media experience.

- Most marketers actually use social media for creating brand awareness. Many find it useful for increasing community engagement and getting more website clicks.

- The best ways to influence people on social media, in decreasing order of impact, are: being responsive, offering promotions, providing educational content, sharing interesting visuals, being funny, offering exclusive content, providing behind-the-scene content.

- The following were found to be the actions on the part of businesses that make people unfollow them (in decreasing order of impact): sending too many promotional messages, sending irrelevant messages, too much tweeting, use of unsuitable slang, being too quiet, not replying.

A Statista [https://www.statista.com] study of 2017 found that a big percentage of marketers felt that social media activities for business offered a high RoI (=return on investment) and many felt that paid promotion on social media too resulted in a very positive RoI. In fact, a good percentage of marketers gave these a higher ranking for RoI than to SEO, content marketing, search engine marketing and email marketing.

A strong correlation between social network usage and online shopping has been found: the more people use social networking platforms, the more they go for shopping online.

Commenting on a Global Overview report by WeAreSocial, Hootsuite, a social media management firm [https://www.hootsuite.com] has noted that social media continues to grow as a source of information about products and brands, and younger demographics are leading these shifts. Even among 55 to 64 year old people, 20% say they have used social networks when researching products and services… Emerging markets lead the way for using social at every step of their digital buying journey.

It was found in a study commissioned by Twitter in 2016 [ref 71] that one in four new vehicle purchasers in the US used Twitter as an input to their vehicle purchase decision.

On the rising expectations of consumers in Europe and Latin America and their use of social media for contacting sellers, a 2016 survey published by Altitude [ref 1] gives these insights:

- Over 80% of customers expected a company to respond within 24 hours after posting on social media.

- 1 in 5 customers used social media to contact a company.

- 29% of customers younger than 34 years contacted suppliers via Facebook.

On the same aspect, a Sproutsocial study of 2017 [ref 64] found the following:

- 4 in 5 consumers feel that social media had made brands accountable.

- 46% of consumers use social media to 'call out' brands or make a complaint.

- No or unsatisfactory response hurts the company in many ways. People who research products online are significantly influenced by negative reviews or comments. On the other hand, helpful response from a brand can quickly turn someone who started out complaining into a positive advocate.

- 70% of those who complain on social media do so for raising public awareness and 55% to get a resolution or response.

EuroStat [ref 30] says that in 2019, 53 % of EU enterprises used at least one type of social media, with more than eight out of ten of these businesses (86 %) using social media to build their image and to market products. The use of social media between 2013 and 2019 increased most for marketing purposes (from 22 % to 45 % of enterprises) and for recruiting employees (from 9 % to 28 % of enterprises).

A large number of employers now use social media for recruitment. LinkedIn is a platform that particularly suits employers in finding talent, and employees in finding jobs. Other platforms where people freely share their opinions are found useful by recruiters for checking the character and conduct of potential employees.

In a 2018 survey [ref 18], CareerBuilder found that in the US,

- 70 percent of employers used social networking sites to research job candidates during hiring process;

- 48 percent of employers checked up on current employees on social media; and

- 34 percent of employers had reprimanded or fired an employee based on content found online.

How social media-savvy businesses actually use it

Businesses of today, except personal shops, cannot run without a presence on social media. This has been clear to all businesses but not all have been found using this important tool efficiently.

Since consumers now have high expectations from businesses (of quick response, instant chatting, posting of response on social media, visual presentation of products, quick resolution of grievance, etc.), any slackness on social media accounts can be counter-productive. Therefore, many firms have their social media guidelines for staff and many get their staff trained on the use of social media.

Progressive companies make social media a key component of their marketing strategy. Big companies that appreciate the potential of social media and can spend huge sums on it have sizable social media teams independent of media/ public relations teams. Their social media teams not only have staff for content creation, analytics, engagement, response to feedback and other core activities, they also hire experts in the areas of sociology and psychology to ensure big impact of their messages.

Social media and chat platforms are also used for marketing and sales purposes. It is seen that large corporations have their internal networks but smaller ones are now using WhatsApp and other communication/

video-conferencing apps for internal communication. Sales teams of big firms, delivery teams of e-commerce firms and small businessmen/ retailers/ freelancers make the best use of apps popular in their locations for making contacts, offering services, announcing special offers, promoting products and after-sale service.

Social Media Platforms Best Suited for Businesses

Not all social media platforms or all types of messages suit all businesses. The peculiarities of social media platforms are a major factor; some are suited more for personal socialization while some at the other end of the spectrum (e.g. LinkedIn, Ryze, and Xing) are honed for business/ professional networking.

The type of business/ product also dictates the suitability of a platform for that particular business. For example, Instagram and Pinterest suit businesses that deal with celebrity/ visual content.

Another very important determinant is the type of *publics* being targeted. Thus, business-to-business (B2B) networking is a different ball game from business-to-consumer (B2C) networking. Since professionals and managers use LinkedIn, this is the social platform of choice for B2B social networking also. On the other hand, Twitter and chat apps can broadcast messages far and wide and get quick reactions, and are widely used for B2C socialization.

People of different genders, age groups, educational levels, socio-economic strata and locations tend to prefer particular social media platforms. For example, Pinterest and Instagram are frequented by women more than men; Facebook is used by older people too in good numbers while Instagram and Snapchat are used predominantly by the younger lot; LinkedIn is much more likely to be used by managers; YouTube videos in English languages (as compared to those in local languages) are more likely to be visited by the higher income group; short-video sharing apps like TikTok and are more popular among those with lower incomes and not comfortable in English; and so on. Businesses do and should focus on platforms on which their existing and potential customers are in large numbers.

It is not that firms use one platform exclusively and ignore others. A firm may be using one platform for customer service and another one for brand building. CMI [ref 24] reports that of the B2B content marketers it surveyed in 2020, 95% used LinkedIn, 86% used Twitter, 83% used Facebook, 53% used YouTube and 46% used Instagram *organically*. In addition, most of them also used paid versions of these platforms. A majority of them used 2 or more platforms. Posts on social networking platforms and blogs were the most used types of content by the marketers it surveyed.

On the other hand, different firms that deal with the same product may use different platforms based on their special circumstances, in-house expertise and experience.

Sometimes even the same social media platform has different products to focus on personal and business requirements. For example, Facebook's *timeline* is mostly used for personal socialization while Facebook *pages* are used mainly for business and professional purposes.

With the realization that customers do not operate in exclusive compartments such as buying through only one of the available channels (e.g. online sellers and marketplaces, apps, social media or offline stores), more and more companies are adopting *omnichannel* approach towards marketing. This approach synergistically uses many channels – and social media is an important and integral part of this strategy.

Monetization by social media platforms themselves

If social media is online socialization that has taken over the minds of over two-thirds of the global population, it also has, in itself, become a business of an unprecedented level. Not only that, the business is growing at a fast pace year after year.

Look at Facebook. It is now one of the top technology companies in the world, with a market capitalization of over $ 768 billion (as on 15.2.2021). The company has acquired Instagram and WhatsApp – the two highly popular social networks. It earns nearly $30 per user in the US

Initially, everything on Facebook was free. Now its operations are all money-centric. Facebook promotes you if you have a business account and you buy advertisements from it. Otherwise, your Facebook *page* is hardly served to your followers. On your *newsfeed*, it keeps pushing content ostensibly to serve you based on your preferences but in reality, what it serves is some extraneous content, at the cost of content from your network of friends.

The same is the case with others, maybe to a lesser extent in some compartments and more in other areas. Social media giants also goad you to open premium accounts in the name of giving exclusive content and better services. For making money out of free services, they keep pushing advertisements in between content.

As Google has shown, tech giants can make a lot of money by purveying free products but monetizing what a user of free products does not mind, e.g. inserting advertisements inside videos or displaying ads in the sidebar of a blog. All major social media platforms now have a range of advertisement packages that suit different types of customers. Many platforms encourage users to create content and make money; in the process, the platforms are enriched in terms of content, and earn commission on the money earned by users.

Social media platforms have also been quick to leverage their massive traffic for offering non-social-media services. For example, some of the top social media entities have started monetary transactions on their platforms and also have product marketplaces.

Some platforms have plans to issue their own cryptocurrencies.

It is not my argument that these companies should not make money. I am just drawing your attention to the reality that once a social media company becomes successful in attracting traffic, the interests of its promoters and shareholders take precedence over the societal interests. They also do not invest enough on keeping the platform clean of inappropriate content. That would be even more evident when we discuss the ethical aspects in chapters on privacy, safety and crime.

Let me close this point with a question. Social and content sharing networks do provide a platform but they hardly create content; all or almost all content is contributed by users. The network would come to naught if there were no content. Therefore, should all the content-pushing platforms not compensate content creators?

Social Commerce

Selling products and services through social media, called 'social commerce', has been growing fast over the years.

The operation is simple and is like a social media version of direct selling done by global companies (e.g. Amway) through their re-sellers. The social commerce aggregating platform lists products of a large number of manufacturers. A re-seller, who is typically an individual with a large social media base, chooses products and offers them through his social media accounts at a higher retail price, thus earning a margin for himself.

Many social commerce platforms have developed apps in local languages, which work well especially in large countries such as China and India.

Market research company Technavio [https://www.technavio.com] has estimated that the global social commerce market would grow at a compounded annual rate of 30.8% between 2019 and 2024.

Food and beauty/ fashion items, baby products, health care and personal care merchandise and financial services are the main niches in which social commerce is seeing high turnover.

E-wallet company PayPal has stated that 80% of merchants it surveyed in 2017-18 in China, India, Hong Kong, Singapore, Thailand, the Philippines and Indonesia were selling their products through social media.

How do individuals earn through social media

Social media helps individuals earn money through it. References to money-earning streams have come here and there in this book, but for the sake of quick enumeration at one place, let me list the main streams here:

- Putting advertisements (direct ads, CPC ads served through AdSense, affiliate ads, etc.) on one's blog.

- Reviewing others' products on one's blog or other social media space.

- Recommending products or endorsing something, as a social media influencer.

- Promoting and/ or selling one's own products and services such as merchandise, book, SEO services and teaching courses.

- Selling others' products through affiliation or social commerce.

- Creating and selling/ monetizing content, e.g. articles, photographs and videos, through blogs, podcasts, vblogs and content sharing sites.

Social Media Influencers

On the web, the word *'social media influencer'* has gained popularity in recent years. This term is used for describing people with a large following on social media. This term is flashed more in relation to Twitter and Instagram than other platforms.

The claim of social media influencers is that they have a huge herd following them and therefore their word matters a lot when it comes to people buying a product or service. Firms/ advertisers pay them well for issuing promotional messages through their profiles/ pages/ blogs.

Influencers do have big numbers behind them and, naturally, they are likely to get more traffic than those with only a few hundred followers. Advertising on such accounts, thus, is bound to be more visible. Blog monetization through AdSense advertisements and affiliation proves that: people with higher traffic earn well because a large number of their visitors click on advertisements and/ or buy through them.

Beyond that, the real influence of *influencers* is a matter of discussion. Influencers - especially public figures with good fan following – do influence their fans and followers. It has been established that when products or brands are endorsed by public figures with a good image, authority over subject and mass following, people tend to trust the products/ brands and want to emulate them or reach their level of success/ beauty/ health/ social recognition by using the endorsed products. Therefore, advertisers use film and sports personalities and pay them handsomely.

Real-life celebrities have a large following and their followers follow them on social media with passion. Social media connects them with fans, sometimes on real-time basis, and whips the fans' urge to know more about celebrities. Because of this, trivial actions or statements by celebrities sometimes go viral on social media.

Beyond celebrities, there are bloggers and others active on social media who have a large genuine following. They have earned goodwill due to their authentic work, and those in their network take their advice seriously. Brands give high value to such influencers.

However, the influence – in the range of momentary hysteria to lasting influence – may not results in the intended action. Look at the following realities:

- Fake following is used for jacking up one's data. A damning expose carried by The New York Times in 2018 stated that a big industry operates to sell fake followers to politicians and other celebrities all over the world, and that a large number of followers of many known global influencers are fake [ref 22].

- On Twitter, it is seen that people with millions of followers themselves follow millions. That means, the accounts have been followed just for the sake of reciprocation and in turn jacking up followers' numbers. In real life, it is not likely that the person with a million followers would be interested in the content posted by even a fraction of them.

- Mere traffic (or follower count) may not be a good measure of influence. People who follow someone on social media need not follow his or her advice. In fact, a large number of followers of the so-called influencers are their adversaries and those interested in analyzing their data for different purposes.

- When people follow social entities with interesting and entertaining content, their interest is limited to fun. YouTube channels and Facebook accounts of people who share jokes and funny videos are followed by thousands, and the followers are not likely to pay any heed to recommendations made by such accounts.

- Most followers on social media, even if they are not fake, are dormant or have gone fully out of action.

- Influencers are also known to be indiscreet and unethical in their conduct. Celebrities sometimes post messages that would subtly influence their followers and fans into buying merchandise they show off or endorse. Some celebrities of global fame are known to have been penalized for that and yet they keep doing so.

- In 2018, UK's Competition and Markets Authority (CMA) started a probe against major celebrity influencers on social media who were posting misleading messages and advertisements in the garb of innocent messages. Since the British consumer protection law, as much as the American law, has strict provisions against misleading advertisements and non-disclosure of commercial terms, some British celebrities then came out publicly to promise that they would make a clear disclosure when their posts have advertorial content.

- In a sting operation carried out before the 2019 general elections in India, CobraPost [http://www.cobrapost.com] found that second-rung Bollywood actors, singers and comedians with a sizable number of fans on social media were willing to post messages favorable to political parties as their personal opinion, for a hefty fee. Some even quoted Rs. 200 million for an 8-month contract [ref 21].

Content, social media and inbound marketing

In modern marketing parlance, these terms are used quite often. So, a short discussion would be pertinent in this section on the use of social media for business.

Content marketing refers to marketing in which content is used for creating awareness and goodwill among customers and prospective clients towards the brand for getting results such as sales, loyalty and advocacy. The content has to be compelling and should get the desired action at different stages of customer's travel from knowing about the brand to purchase and beyond.

When the focus is on promoting business through the use of compelling content, the firm's website and blog happen to be the main vehicles of long-form content and long videos. Of course, content has to be created for social networking platforms too, but that is often subsidiary content.

Social media marketing refers to the use of social media for marketing purposes. In this context, *social media* refers to both the content that is posted on social media platforms and the medium of communication. Thus, firms create special messages for social media and serve them through a well thought-after strategy. At the same time, they use the vehicle of social media to purvey content and provide services. The overall social media marketing strategy includes all methods of using social media for promotion, sale and customer service.

What is seen is that content and social media marketing overlap to a great extent. The content used on social networking and instant messaging platforms often acts as a hook to induce the users towards the long-form content on websites and blogs. Of course, there are actions on social media that do not need too much focus on content (e.g. engagement) and there are many other channels for serving good content besides social media and websites (e.g. email, print).

Let me repeat that social media has become a very important part of marketing strategies adopted by businesses because present as well as prospective customers are likely to be active on social media platforms. Of course, social media marketing achieves success only when the content is trustworthy, of high quality and customized for individual platforms. There cannot be a uniform strategy for all social media platforms, and therefore big firms have strategies specific to major platforms, e.g. Facebook marketing and Instagram marketing.

Inbound marketing refers to the act of convincing prospects to take favorable action when they like something about the brand. Unlike *outbound* marketing, e.g. advertisement, in which you try to convince people to like your brand and make a purchase, in inbound marketing strategy you serve them the content while they seek a solution and then – you *pull* the prospective client *in*. Therefore, content is of paramount importance in inbound marketing, and social media is an important medium for publishing that content. That way, this also overlaps with the other two marketing streams mentioned above.

As applies to mainstream marketing, social media marketing should not look like *marketing*. In this respect, social media can be unsparing. If the marketing messages are inappropriate, too frequent or intrusive, or targeted wrongly, they may backfire much more and quicker than such messages/ content on the traditional media (newspapers, magazines, television, etc.).

USE OF SOCIAL MEDIA IN DEMOCRATIC POLITICS AND ELECTIONS

The web is full of news items and study reports that suggest that social media has become an important battle-ground for politics, and may be influencing all elections held in the last 15 years in many ways. Its influence, good or bad or mixed, is increasing year by year not only because social media consumption is increasing but also due to other factors such as its cost-effectiveness and availability of sophisticated analytical tools.

The first major use of social media in elections was seen in the 2008 US Presidential election. In elections and referenda held after that in democracies across the continents, such as the UK, France, Germany, Brazil, Australia, India and Zimbabwe, and three subsequent elections held in the US, have witnessed intense use of social media during elections.

About the US presidential elections of 2008, it was reported that about half of the voting population used online platforms for getting election-related information and to connect with the election process. Among internet users, about 59% used instant messaging or text messaging tools or Twitter for receiving or giving campaign-related information.

According to a study by Pew Research Center [ref 61], about 18% of internet users had posted a political commentary online using one of the many options available: on a social networking site, on a website that allowed commenting and discussion, on one's own or others' blogs, or in an online discussion (e.g. on a forum).

It is also said that part of the credit for the win of Barack Obama in that election goes to his online political activism. It is also stated that with the help of social media he was able to connect well with the younger population. A point to note is that in 2008, social networking platforms were yet evolving.

In the 2014 parliamentary election in India, social media became a fierce battleground. A large mobile-first population had entered the digital world through social networking, unlike the majority in advanced countries who graduated from websites to blogs to social networking. Besides, a significant part of India's population was young as compared to western nations. Narendra Modi, whose party came to power with a landslide victory in that election, understood the power of social media to spread his brand, especially among young and aspirational Indians. On the other hand, many old-styled politicians had, at that time, ridiculed social media platforms and considered social media engagement a waste of time. In all, social media was recognized as a new medium, which - even if it was not sure to influence voting - was more cost-effective in projecting a candidate and his views than some other types of media.

In the 2016 US presidential election, the winner (Donald Trump) and his close competitor (Hillary Clinton) were covered well by the traditional media. However, the third candidate, Bernie Sanders, was not covered or was covered condescendingly by the media; yet he was able to garner significant voter support on the back of a high social media presence. Of course, Trump used his tweets – quirky, witty and often offensive and controversial – that gave him huge social media coverage and following. Trump publicly shared that social media helped him win the primary and general elections even though his opponents spent much more money than him on traditional media advertising.

Since 2008, the changes in social media have been incremental only: new platforms have arisen and some have gone down, and the role of social media in people's lives has increased significantly. But when it comes to elections, social media has graduated from a means of reaching and influencing people to a political battlefield. It is not an option any longer to use or not use social media; in some countries, social media has become a more important part of election management than traditional media. There is also little doubt now about social media's influence on the political discourse. In the lower sections, I discuss this all from different angles.

What purpose does social media serve during elections

There are several players that have an integral role in democratic elections, and debates, outreach and preparations before and after elections. The main players – other than the voters - are the political formations and politicians, the election authorities and their implementation machinery, and even miscreants and interested foreign actors. Now that social media has become the best medium for information dissemination and communication, it serves many functions.

Political parties and candidates seek to achieve the following through social media:

- Creating a brand for individual politicians and their political parties.

- Constantly updating committed voters and well-wishers, and supplying them with positive news worth sharing.

- Reaching potential voters.

- Creating a positive buzz for oneself on social media by constantly posting positive news and info-nuggets.

- Explaining one's stand on different policy matters and emerging political developments.

- Responding to issues, especially those raised by opponents.

- Creating a negative image of opponents by sharing their weaknesses and wrongdoings.

- Spreading disinformation about opponents and reinforcing negative news already circulating about them.

- Fund-raising.

- Damage control, by presenting one's side when harmful content comes on media/ social media, explaining away one's loss in the election, etc.

- Mobilizing voters/ supporters for physical action, e.g. attending a public meeting or actually voting (instead of remaining at home).

Election bodies the world over have been making good use of social media for different purposes. These include:

- Internal communication, especially when they do not have internal communication facilities.

- Encouraging people to participate in elections.

- Cautioning people against election-related misinformation.

- Giving positive messages that strengthen public confidence in the election system.

- Issuing and sending election-related updates.

Social media is being used by groups or foreign governments/ agencies that have a vested interest in spoiling the democratic process. This trend, as we will discuss later, has threatened the sanctity of many countries in recent years. The main motivations behind this are:

- Impairing the election process, to create suspicion in the system itself.

- Using elections to create disharmony in the society.

- Favoring the prospects of one political formation and hurting the interests of its opponents.

- Spreading misinformation on behalf of domestic players and committing election-related frauds from servers outside the country because the legal or administrative authorities of that country have no control over them.

How politicos use social media

Political parties and individual politicians use different platforms for setting agendas and driving discussions on specific issues during elections; Facebook, Twitter and instant messaging platforms seem to be the most preferred ones. Some of the most followed accounts on Facebook and Twitter belong to national political leaders, showing the importance of social media in spreading their messages far and wide.

Lay politicians use social media based on their common-sense (or of the person helping them out with social media engagements) and guided by their whims. They are interested in getting a big follower-count, sometimes in unethical ways such as creating fake accounts or buying followers. They spread their party's social media messages, sometimes adding their own comments. The idea is to be seen as active and in a favorable light on social media. When it comes to connecting with their own constituency, many of them seem to do better by introducing themselves, offering to help with voter registration, sending alerts about voting dates, etc. But they have neither expert advice on social media, nor sophisticated tools or other resources.

On the other hand, major political parties and top politicians, especially in major democracies, have taken to social media in a very professional manner, customizing it and leveraging its potential for reaching and influencing people at universal, constituency, booth and voter levels.

It has been documented that big political parties and their leaders, especially when they are in power, have great machinery at their disposal for dominating the social media scene. However, when that happens, people take the role of the adversary even when there is no big political opposition present. That in a way 'balances' the power equilibrium on social media. However, this cannot happen when the freedom to use social media is suppressed through illegitimate use of administrative or legal power.

Most political leaders and parties have their back-end teams that create content, quickly share and re-share it on social media using a large number of accounts, artificially create buzz, react to opponents' content and engage in fight and trolling against the opponents' followers. An army of workers is raised to do this work at a higher scale in the months preceding a major election.

Reaching political followers and well-wishers is of prime importance for political parties and politicians. Social media provides a very powerful medium for not only *reach* but also *outreach* to this section. Social media has great potential in this area because people with the same political views and affiliations tend to make their own groups on social network platforms. In addition, fans and followers do not need much incentive to act favorably on social media. Therefore, not much effort is required to reach this group or to make them spread the politician's or party's messages on social media.

Fans and supporters also tend to mirror physical campaigning on social media. Those attending campaigns and getting a chance to take photos and videos of top political leaders share them on their social media accounts to show off their political activism or closeness with political leaders. They also share whatever positive comes on social media or elsewhere relating to the party and candidate of their choice. Many hardcore fans indulge in trolling, spreading disinformation and other forms of online abuse.

Then comes reaching the fence-sitters and those with opposite political views or affiliations. They can be won over only through sustained campaign, both positive and negative, and promise of public or personal benefits that party or candidate of their allegiance cannot deliver. In negative campaigning, they need to be shown how their candidate or party is going to hurt their own or public interests – and the promise that I or my party would not let that happen. Therefore, the carrot and/ or stick needs to be dangled craftily before such people.

Social media has the promise, much more than traditional media, to target messages that would strike the bull. Tools are available to know the online behavior, likes and dislikes, memorability and other attributes of a large population and to analyze it. Tools are also available to then deliver specific messages in the right way to specific target groups. The targeting of messages to small groups on social media, called micro-targeting, is now an important part of the strategy adopted by political social media management firms.

No other online activity generates as much data and none can beat social media in targeting messages to specific audiences. Big social media platforms are willing to sell private data to companies engaged in mind-manipulation who in turn work for political parties or foreign agencies.

It is also reported that political parties in some countries themselves have social media infrastructure that captures and analyzes data, and spreads messages using sophisticated technological tools, and a big back-end team.

Before the 2016 US presidential election, Cambridge Analytica, a British firm engaged in political advertising and political counseling, made Facebook users' psychological profiles and used the data for swaying undecided voters in favor of Donald Trump. This very firm claimed that it was using social media data in the elections of at least one Indian state for many years till 2013.

Though more elections have been held in the US and India after 2016, the way Narendra Modi and Donald Trump used social media in their national elections in 2014 and 2016 are relevant for the present discussion. These leaders understood the potential of social media much before the start of their political campaigns and before others appreciated its potential. They used social media for connecting with the masses directly and with messages that resonated with public sentiment at that time. Both had the advantage of being in the opposition and thus amplify the disenchantment or fatigue with the ruling formations. While Modi was persuasive, Trump used provocation to achieve a deep connect with fans and voters. Not surprisingly, Trump rode the wave of social media till he was banned or suspended by major social media platforms in 2021 after his provocative tweets. Modi tops the list of world leaders in terms of followers on different social media platforms. Being the Prime Minister now, he has the task to keep the trust of the people in what he is doing, much less than criticizing what his opponents do – and his social media engagements seem to be achieving that.

If social media helps national leaders to reach their fan-base and beyond, local leaders are getting equally adept at the use of social media. Often, the platforms of choice differ. For example, local politicians use location-specific or interest-specific groups on messaging apps much more than national leaders. In big countries, some local social media apps have emerged that speak the local tongue, and are thus able to connect with voters better than big platforms such as Twitter and Facebook.

Social media offers a great opportunity for local leaders to connect with the population: listening to their views and problems and offering solutions – not only during elections.

The use of social media in elections is highly cost-effective in many ways. One, just posting on social network platforms does not cost a dime, and the messages are shared and broadcast by people at no cost to the political leader or his party. Two, maintaining own social media team or hiring an agency for social media campaigning multiplies one's online presence considerably with a low investment. Three, political advertising on social media is much cheaper than that on mainstream media. Four, since one can target social media messages and advertisements to specific groups, the cost in terms of reaching the message to the target audiences comes further down.

The low cost, high reach, more engagement and the possibility of quick results associated with social media have convinced politicos to advertise online – on websites and social media. A look at the Facebook Ad Library project [ref 32] shows that political, politically-oriented or indirect ads supporting a political cause keep being run throughout the year and irrespective of elections. As is expected, their quantity increased in months before elections. Between July and October 2020, Biden Victory Fund spent $53 million and Trump Make America Great Again Committee $39.8 million on Facebook ads alone. Between February and May 2019, Facebook received Rs.292.8 million through political ads in India.

Whether social media really makes an impact on election outcomes?

Before we come to whether social media makes an impact on election outcomes, let us very briefly see how it influences political democracy in general.

Some experts have argued that social media has not only been vitiating elections but undermining democracy *in toto* by its partisan and prejudiced social engagements and not allowing healthy and informed debate on core issues. Many political, economic, security, diplomatic and social issues are extremely complex and there may be valid arguments for and against an action; in such cases, a mature debate is necessary for not only people's vote on such issues but also for a considered decision by an elected government. However, on social media people only reinforce an opinion that they are in love with and do not want to listen to other voices. Thus, multi-dimensional matters of national interest too become bipartisan issues and if you are on one side, you are the enemy of the other. Though this was an old hypothesis, the 2020 US elections have proved it. Let me hasten to add here that social media is only a *tool* for social and political polarization; the fault lies elsewhere.

On the other hand, several political observers look optimistically at the huge potential of social media in broad-basing and encouraging political discussion, thus contributing to the democratic process. The serious segment of social media (e.g. political blogging, discussions on YouTube channels) can lead to meaningful political discourse. Even transient and emotional political messaging on social media contributes to political discussion in many ways, e.g. by providing alternative viewpoints, as an additional source of information, giving the power to the common man to express himself, and exposing follies. The noise also makes the politicians – who otherwise may like to ignore minor issues and citizen problems – take notice and respond.

In some studies, it has been found that the younger generation now consumes news more on social media than on traditional media. It is also found that they are influenced by political news that is served to them on social media, and also participate more in the political debate and elections under the influence of social media. The intermediation done by social media platforms, feed aggregators and news apps is important here as much as the creation, mid-way editing and dissemination of content by politicians and people at large.

The initial refusal of social media platforms in taking action against the accounts of Donald Trump when he was propagating divisive content and then banning his account give a taste of the power of social media platforms. In a 2020 study by Pew Research, 72% of US adults said that social media companies have too much power and influence in politics.

Political thinkers have used these examples to raise a concern about their capacity over the population and argued that this might undermine democracy unless a mechanism is found for checking their powers. At the same time, the question is, who will do the oversight? Governments cannot be trusted with this role. Perhaps courts and election authorities can become too restrictive in applying rules and norms. Some people are not ready for a United Nations system for this, saying that it can be pliable to pressure from powerful nations. As of now, a mix of all these checks, in addition to active pressure from some legislative bodies and self-regulation seem to be working, though falteringly. Some fear its rampant abuse by governments and other state-actors in future elections. On the other hand, some sociologists stick to the hope that social media will get politically mature in the years to come.

Coming to social media's impact on election outcomes, most research literature is based on impressionistic surveys, and therefore more empirical studies are needed for making strong conclusions. Yet some plausible inferences can be drawn.

Some research on the impact of social media on political behavior shows that social media is more of a reinforcing force rather than being able to alter voting preferences. It has been found that more than a real influencer, social media creates echo chambers, closed communities in which people have the same views, promote the same content, denounce any opposing view, and be happy that their view is the one that is valid and getting a good audience.

On the other hand, studies also show that social media does influence people's opinions, though to a small extent. In a survey quoted elsewhere in detail [ref 56], it was found that 7% of US social media users polled in 2020 (the year of election) had changed their opinion about Donald Trump and 11% about political parties, ideologues, etc. [usually after social media engagements and further checking facts].

It is not clear whether the social media dominance of an opinion or a candidate influences public opinion and voting, by 'bandwagon effect' as is supposed to be a case in real life. An expert observation [ref 14]: "… these numbers were artificially inflated - millions of those followers were fake, after all. But he was right. Regardless of how bogus the traffic was, it did something more important. It created a bandwagon effect among actual voters and legitimized fringe views that turned out to be supported by a lot of people. Consequently, whatever was being shared had to be taken more seriously by journalists, and their coverage then broadcast those stories—some of them fake, it would turn out—even more widely."

It has also been observed that social media encourages people to vote. Peer pressure seems to work especially on young people when their friends post on social media the photos of their having cast the vote.

Political parties and candidates use social media tools to keep persuading voters to vote in their favor and alert them about the approaching date. They also mobilize people by spreading fear that followers of the opposite side have voted in large numbers. Empirical studies have proved that in the 2014 Indian elections, young people voted in large numbers under the influence of social media.

In recent elections in major democracies, social media's influence looks certain; I am, however, not sure about the extent of influence. A common observation is that social media may not have a considerable positive impact, but it does its job well in damaging candidates' prospects.

The use of social media on election outcomes should not be a one-time affair. Yet, it so happens that political leaders and parties try to connect with their constituents and potential followers while campaigning or just before that. Many politicians and political parties are seen doing so in real life as well as on social media. This leaves a big credibility gap, and however noisy the campaign may become, it is not likely to win voters' minds.

It is also seen that the quality of social messages is often ignored due to obsession with numbers and popularity on social media. Many campaigns on social media usually look aloof and condescending. Such social media campaigns are not able to connect the politician with social media users at a personal level. Some politicians indulge in too much negative campaigning – dwelling on the weaknesses, inglorious family history, and acts of omission and commission of the opponent. While such a campaign might (perhaps, and in certain situations) get support and reinforcement when pitched before a receptive crowd, it is likely to boomerang on social media because by its very nature it can be very unpardoning.

Aberrations in the use of social media in politics and elections

The quality of political discourse on social media is generally of low quality, being unreasonable, intolerant and angry, hitting below the belt, even getting threatening, libelous and abusive. It gets more vitiated as the election day approaches. There seems to be a strong notion among political parties and leaders that a cacophonous buzz needs to be created to drown the voice of the opposition and that the noise sways the public opinion in one's favor. Desperation on the part of the contestants is seen to further degrade it. It often gets out of control due to the interplay of messages in the hands of political formations and followers.

It has been observed that in all political elections, election campaigning is more virulent on social media than on other channels (physical or virtual debates, rallies, traditional media, outdoor media, pamphlets, etc.).

All types of dirty technology-mediated tricks are used to boost one's actions and disparage others'. The sad reality is that a large part of political content being shared and forwarded on social media during elections is engineered or fake, and most comments and likes are not genuine.

Often a large number of other interests are at play; these include interested criminals, terrorists, enemy countries, intelligence agencies, and industry/ trade lobbies.

Inimical foreign governments and their agencies, or operators that find a safe haven in such countries, can be big players in elections. The mingling by Russian entities in the 2016 US presidential elections is proved beyond doubt. Declassified documents have revealed that fake accounts, manipulative messaging, mass sharing of messages, trolls and paid dis-information were used in addition to state-funded media, media intermediaries and other non-social media players. Facebook has admitted that at least 80,000 posts were published on its platform by Russian actors, and these reached 126 million people in the US over a two-year period.

In its 2020 report, Twitter has named a number of countries whose state-actors regularly tried to disrupt conversations on the platform during the year and it took action against them. These include China, Russia, Turkey, Serbia, Honduras, Egypt, Indonesia, Ghana and Nigeria. There were serious allegations that Pakistani entities were involved in the 2018 provincial elections in India.

A cyber-attack before Australia's federal elections in 2019 on computer networks of parliament and three political parties was attributed to Chinese state security; Russian agencies are supposed to have attacked Ukraine's election commission servers in 2019 ahead of the 2019 presidential elections; political attacks using Twitter are supposed to be engineered in a neighboring country during 2018 Swedish elections; Russia-supported agencies are reported to have been active on Twitter, Facebook and YouTube during 2019 European Parliament elections; Russian military induced phishing of US Senate think-tanks was noticed in 2018 midterm elections... The list of suspected attempts by foreign-based agents, though all of them are not proven, to manipulate social media for political reasons is virtually unending.

Cambridge Analytica's mingling in the elections of some countries is a damning example of how deeply the misinformation-machinery can undermine legitimate political processes.

One major aberration in the use of social media in politics/ elections is the spread of fake news especially in the months preceding a major election. Fake news has become an industry in itself; about $400 million is spent on political fake news, according to a 2019 estimate [ref 8].

The generation and spread of fake news for political purposes follow the same patterns as for other purposes. Please visit <u>Misinformation and fake news</u> section in <u>Social Media as Mass Media and Medium of Free Expression</u> chapter for a detailed discussion on this biggest malady of social media.

Political fake news is generated by political parties and politicians, their supporters and other interested parties as mentioned above. These actors usually do not get involved in social media manipulation for the fun of it but have an interest in the win or defeat of one among the contestants. While all of them take every opportunity to make the best of the mistakes or follies committed by the other side, the main actors use psychological tools to turn even the most genuine positive information into a damaging piece.

It is not that fake news is spread with negative content only, political formations in power, and also their governmental, intelligence and defense agencies, churn out fake news in the form of exaggerated facts and figures, and fallacious arguments for bloating the achievement of the government and its key functionaries. With the government's powers and resources in hand, the sheer quantity of information or misinformation that the ruling formation can push on social media has the potential to drown the opposite viewpoints. However, as mentioned earlier, social media has a quality to create an equilibrium of sort in which common users tend to push opposite viewpoints, something that cannot happen on uni-directional traditional media.

A Pew Research survey found that about three-fourths of US voters felt that in the 2016 election, fake news caused a great deal of confusion about the basic facts of current issues and events [ref 47]. Another study showed that fake news consumption during that election had a significant political bias, with Conservatives consuming much more fake news than Liberals. Trump supporters were also found to be users of fake news in much higher quantities than Clinton supporters. There are also studies that suggest that fake news definitely made an impact on the 2016 US elections, though it might have been too small to contribute to the final victory of Donald Trump.

But the 2020 US presidential election broke all boundaries in the spread of fake news. The campaign itself was highly vitriolic, with Trump supporters trashing all Biden claims of leading, and Biden supporters and Trump haters organizing rallies against Trump on his dealing with the COVID-19 pandemic and a strong rightist stand taken by him on many matters.

The bitter social media fight continued even after the election results were announced, resulting in social media platforms taking action against Trump and his followers.

Trump has been active on Twitter so much so that his official views were first shared on his Twitter account than on official channels. In January 2021, a fortnight before he was to demit office as US President, Twitter 'permanently suspended the account [of Trump] due to the risk of further incitement of violence'. Trump had been tweeting, calling the counting of postal ballots in the presidential election fraud, then asking supporters to not accept the results, then saying that he won't give up at any cost.

In the same period, Facebook imposed 'indefinite suspension' on Trump's accounts from Facebook and Instagram, stating that his messages incited violence and thronging of the Capitol. It then referred the matter to its Oversight Board - an expert-led independent organization with the power to impose binding decisions on Facebook. The statement issued by Facebook on its blog is a quotable commentary on the role and responsibilities of social media in such situations: "…In open democracies people have a right to hear what their politicians are saying - the good, the bad and the ugly - so that they can be held to account. But it has never meant that politicians can say whatever they like. They remain subject to our policies banning the use of our platform to incite violence... Whether you believe the decision was justified or not, many people are understandably uncomfortable with the idea that tech companies have the power to ban elected leaders. Many argue private companies like Facebook shouldn't be making these big decisions on their own… It would be better if these decisions were made according to frameworks agreed by democratically accountable lawmakers. But in the absence of such laws, there are decisions that we cannot duck."

Other social media platforms followed suit, ignominiously ending the grip of a powerful but irresponsible social media influencer.

Among other concerns about that election, one can count the proliferation of fake news on social media in pre-election days and virulent anti-immigration campaigns on social media. It is assessed that at least 5% of tweets were generated through bots.

Many failed and successful cyber-attacks to undermine elections were noted in recent French and German elections. It is established that foreign players and servers in foreign countries tried to repeatedly manipulate social media engagement in many European nations during elections in the last ten years despite their being exposed.

The extent of fake news spread in different elections may vary. An analysis of Twitter data by Grinberg *et al* [ref 37] showed that fake news accounted for just 6% of all news consumption during the 2014 US elections, and it was heavily concentrated. Only 1% of users were exposed to 80% of fake news, and 0.1% of users were responsible for sharing 80% of fake news. "Individuals most likely to engage with fake news sources were of conservative leaning, older, and highly engaged with political news. A cluster of fake news sources shared overlapping audiences on the extreme right, but for people across the political spectrum, most political news exposure still came from mainstream media outlets." A much higher percentage of users are likely to be exposed to fake news now.

Brazilian newspaper Folha carried a detailed report on how social media played a big role in screwing up the 2018 Brazilian election. A number of tools and use of social media data for targeting messages are reported to have been used for generating damning content against political rivals [ref 33]. Some parties are supposed to have used disinformation and fake news through social media to poison voters' minds against adversaries.

Brazilian newspapers have especially taken note of a disinformation campaign on WhatsApp to discredit the winning candidate's rival. The campaign, financed by a business lobby and fueled by the supporters of the winning candidate (Bolsonaro, the new President), is said to have spread doctored photographs, selectively edited audio clips and circulated false 'fact-checks'.

In 2017, the Philippines President indirectly admitted that he had spent thousands of dollars on trolls to defend him during elections in the previous year.

In a sting operation conducted in 2018-19 in India [ref 21], many celebrities accepted the offer to publish, for a hefty fee, politically favorable messages on their social media accounts.

Another way of manipulating political opinion using social media is political advertising. While a major part of it is direct, and transparent to that extent, some is covert. Paid news is one form of paid content, in which the paid content or advertisement are served in the garb of news or feature articles. Election bodies take the help of technology and platforms so that money power does not unduly influence public opinion. However, they do not succeed well because new ways of bypassing the system are discovered and unclear rules and legal loopholes are exploited. As the spending on social media is difficult to monitor, candidates can bypass the spending limits fixed by election authorities, as seen in the 2017 UK election and 2019 Indian election. In the 2019 Philippines elections, it was noticed that social media influencers, more so with a lower number of followers and those creating memes and sexually suggestive videos and pop music were used to spread political messages for skirting the spending limits.

In 2019, Twitter banned political ads on the platforms, declaring, "Ads that contain references to political content, including appeals for votes, solicitations of financial support, and advocacy for or against any of the above-listed types of political content, are prohibited under this policy" [ref 72]. Some other platforms including Pinterest and LinkedIn stopped accepting political ads. However, the biggest social network, Facebook, has chosen to keep accepting political ads, though it was Facebook on which Russian government-funded ads were used for political messaging during the 2016 US presidential elections. One step, however, that the platform has taken is to make political advertising transparent (see below for more details).

Efforts by social media platforms towards free and fair elections

Let me end this section with some recent actions that social media platforms have taken or promised to be taking towards using social media for supporting free and fair elections and checking its misuse during elections.

In successive elections worldwide in recent years, major social networks and other tech giants including Google and Microsoft are seen taking initiatives – mostly in conjunction with national governments, election bodies and NGOs – towards making their platforms clean and responsible.

Election authorities themselves have been giving social media high priority in their scheme of things. National election authorities take major social media platforms in their fold for voter literacy and support, disseminating election-related information and checking misinformation. They also issue guidelines to be followed by social media platforms during elections. Major social media platforms set up teams for election-related work and create resource pages to show the actions being taken by them according to the guidelines. Some social media platforms also financially support research on the topics relating to social media use in elections.

An understanding was reached between the Indian election commission and social media platforms before the 2019 elections, and the platforms committed to take down any content that violated the election code of conduct, within three hours. All social media platforms also obliged by appointing a grievance officer who was responsible for taking immediate action on complaints of misuse of that platform during elections.

Major social networks such as Facebook have put it on record on their websites that they have been supporting fragile democracies in Africa and other parts of the globe with resources and expertise.

The efforts by social media platforms seem to succeed but only to an extent. In some cases, they are seen to be 'not doing enough'. Sometimes, their efforts do not succeed despite big efforts. They are also blamed to be taking a biased position.

Twitter, TikTok, LinkedIn and Pinterest have stopped taking political advertising on their platforms. Facebook and Google have argued that political promotion in any form should be acceptable as long as it is not illegal, and they allow political ads. Facebook has sought to be transparent about the political ads being carried on the platform by listing such ads in its Ad Library [ref 32]. Google says it restricts micro-targeting in the pre-election period.

The above was only a glimpse of the working of social media in politics and elections. Please note that every country's socio-political make-up and also its social media user profile and behavior are unique. What I have tried is to bring forth key observations and trends seen in major democracies. Media is full of highly critical reports about the use of social media by powerful political formations, they have been avoided except a few unavoidable mentions because this book is not meant to be a political document.

USE OF SOCIAL MEDIA BY GOVERNMENTS

The use of social media by governments is almost equally varied as its use by individuals. At one end of the spectrum, some government institutions have been proactive from the early days of blogging for bringing online services to citizens and engaging with them, and at the other end, there are governments that abhor social media. Whatever their sentiment towards it, governments the world over are obsessed with social media and try to tame it for meeting their goals.

Governments' handling of social media as an adversary

I have discussed this subject in detail in <u>Concerns Relating to Safety & Security, Privacy and Government Control</u> chapter.

Governments' use of social media for providing information and services

Governments and public service organizations can fruitfully use social media for the following (and many more) purposes:

- Informing people about their rights and public services available to them.

- Announcing new facilities and explaining their provisions.

- Delivering services to citizens.

- Clarifying government's policies, especially on major subjects and issues.

- Seeking people's views in policy formulation.

- Seeking feedback on programs, and involving people in monitoring them.

- Eliciting people's participation in the implementation of government programs.

- Advising/ cautioning people against emerging social, health or economic issues.

- Communication in time of emergencies.

While there are shining examples of the use of social media usefully by public bodies (we shall visit some of them in the next pages), it is observed that governments are generally not efficient in making use of social media. This is due to many reasons such as lop-sided prioritization, poor understanding of social media and lack of commitment by top functionaries. Hierarchy, aloofness and resistance or fear in changing procedures come as big hindrances in the effective use of social media by government agencies as social media engagement demands informal exchanges and quick responses.

Let me stress that lack of intent rather than limitations of social media tools is what results in poor use of social media by governments. After all, social media is an optional tool and if there is not enough commitment on the part of governmental agencies towards solving people's problems, improving efficiencies and reducing citizen-bureaucrat interface, the tool cannot be expected to achieve great results. In many cases, some government departments and agencies seem to be on social media because they are forced to or because others are already there, and in such cases, there is no commitment on the part of the leadership. The lower-end functionaries are not initiated, trained, and most importantly – not encouraged and guided – in the use of social media. Therefore, social media accounts are opened and forgotten, or they are used for broadcasting information. Instead of having citizen-centric content, social media accounts are often full of speeches and visuals of the top gun and his routine activities are projected as glorious achievements.

Many governments (and their appendages) look at social media as a tool for propaganda rather than using it for citizen-centric services. In that role, governments are found to be abusing social media in many ways. Covert as well as overt agencies of governments, especially those run by autocratic and corrupt rulers, use social media to spread lies and exaggerations about the achievements of the top functionaries. A look at the reports coming in the media all over the world shows that most governments are guilty of misuse of social media – and that is no surprise because disinformation seems to be intrinsic to statecraft.

Globally, the use of social media for policy discussion and raising governance issues remains low, possibly due to governments themselves not wanting to educate citizens or induce them towards informed debates. This may in turn be because once people are encouraged to speak on governance matters, political returns are not guaranteed but inefficiencies and flaws in governance are more likely to be exposed. Besides, which government wants to give handles for scrutiny to its political opponents?

It has also been observed that while the political heads of governments and other policymakers tend to gain a following on social media over time, the following of many important offices such as welfare offices and emergency response agencies, do not rise as much. The main reason for such poor appeal for the social accounts of useful services is their indifference towards online socialization, inefficiency comes next.

A US Congress paper of 2016 [ref 23] admits to the failure of that institution to adapt to social media: "As society changes, Congress has stood still. Innovations in technology have revolutionized how people communicate with one another, yet Congress by and large still operates the same way it did in the 1960s. The result: offices find themselves unable to handle ever-increasing volumes of communications, critical knowledge cannot be shared promptly, and staff experience unnecessary frustration, stress, and burnout. The institution itself has been weakened. How can Congress transform itself to better meet the demands of the Information Age?"

In a 2018 study made by GovLoop [ref 36] among the government sector workforce in the US, it was found that only 40 percent felt that their agency had a clear social media strategy. Their usage of efficient social media tools was quite low. Yet, over half of respondents said that the use of social media has resulted in a better understanding of citizens' needs, and positive sentiment. A lesser number felt that this led to good press, better attendance at local events, ability to make informed decisions and faster adoption of changes in services.

In the above-mentioned study, the following were found to be the major challenges that inhibit success in the use of social media (in decreasing order of importance):

- Skill gap/ lack of training

- Lack of cross-departmental collaboration

- Lack of human resource

- Lack of budget

- Inability to measure success

- Departmental resistance

- Approval process

- Increased expectations from citizens

- Trolls

- Lack of centralized ownership

- Lack of buy-in from leadership

- Lack of wide adoption

- Technologies not connected (79% do not have social media integration with other software)

- Industry regulation

Social media tends to be synergistic with other forms of media, and therefore service providers use it with other online and offline tools. Proactive governments have used an integrated set of social media platforms, considering that different platforms have their strengths and weaknesses. It has been observed in the field in OECD nations that social media can bridge gaps still faced by many traditional online government services [ref 45].

With its limitless possibilities of engagement with people, social media can transcend communication barriers and help governments bring in transparency in administration, reach people, elicit their participation and deliver services. Constraints such as poor literacy and low internet penetration in developing countries can be overcome, corruption in governance can be reduced, and costs of services can be pared if governments change their mindset from one-way communication to engaging citizens as valuable stakeholders.

Governments and their agencies in many countries have been using social media and other web tools for talking with and providing services to their citizens. Police have been allowing people to give information on crimes. Traffic police are using ICT tools for getting alerts from the public about traffic congestion, accidents and violation of rules. Many alert citizens help the authorities with not only information but also photographic proof of crime. Education Boards and public recruitment agencies have been listening to students' and applicants' grievances and providing online solutions. Tax authorities are using social media to encourage tax compliance. Municipalities are seeking citizens' help in finding problems relating to garbage collection, leakage, water-logging, etc. The list goes on.

A tool, Advanced Application for Social Media Analytics or AASMA, has been developed by an institute with Indian government funding, which was being used by 40 federal and state government departments in 2017 and 75 were in the queue [ref 60]. The tool is being used for collecting and analyzing live data on users from multiple social networks to find top users, conducting sentiment analysis and other purposes towards bringing efficiency in service delivery.

In a more elevated form of citizen engagement, democratic governments are now sharing their drafts of important bills with people before introducing them in legislatures. Some governments go a step further by engaging people in discussions about those bills. Similarly, administrative actions with likely major effect on social harmony, morality, etc. are often placed on the web before the actions are really taken.

Some governments have tried to involve individuals and communities in policy formulation and governance by encouraging participation in ideation, discussions and actions. Some national and provincial governments that have been active in this field include those of Australia, the USA, UK, EU and OECD, Singapore, South Korea and Canada.

One area that has gained quite significantly through the use of social media and instant messaging is emergency response. Instant messaging apps are now widely used by individuals, communities and agencies for preventive communication, information dissemination and real-time updates, and for delivery of relief and rescue services.

SOCIAL MEDIA ADOPTION BY NON-PROFITS

Non-governmental organizations (NGOs) find social media an inexpensive and efficient tool for furthering their objectives. The first brush of NGOs with social media was through blogging, and to date about 38% of global NGOs maintain a blog. Archives reveal that some big not-for-profit organizations and charities adopted social media even before progressive governments took notice of the new medium.

Non-governmental organizations make use of social media for the following purposes:

- Publicizing their activities and creating a positive image.

- Creating awareness about the social cause for which the NGO works.

- Publicizing events and running publicity campaigns.

- Updating existing donors and well-wishers about its activities; engaging with them.

- Fundraising.

- Recruiting volunteers.

The 'Global NGO Technology Report for 2019' by Nonprofit Tech for Good [ref 49] records big variations in social media adoption by NGOs in different continents. At the global level, its report gives interesting stats:

- 90% of NGOs regularly use social media to engage their supporters and donors.

- 94% agree that social media is effective for online brand awareness, 80% for recruiting event attendees, 78% for creating social change, 75% for recruiting volunteers and inspiring people to take political action, and 72% for online fundraising.

- 84% use Facebook, 46% use Twitter, 42% use Instagram, 28% use LinkedIn, 28% use WhatsApp, 26% use YouTube.

- 44% of NGOs worldwide have a written social media strategy. 42% utilize an editorial calendar for their social media campaigns. 27% have a system in place to track and report return on investment (ROI) on social media campaigns. 80% say that their board helps, rather than hinders, their use of social media.

A 2017 study by Seo and Vu [ref 59] found that international non-profit organizations based in the US have shifted to social media for online communication in a big way over the last ten years. In 2007, they used their websites, followed by blogs, podcasts, video-casts and wikis, but now social media comes just after the website in their list of online channels. Within social media, Facebook comes first, followed by Twitter, blogs and Instagram. The focus of their online communication has also shifted from promoting the organization's image, fund-raising and the media to reaching the general public, potential donors, existing donors and the media in that order. Reaching the media gets a low priority now, the study revealed.

SOCIAL MEDIA AND ACTIVISM

Activism runs on emotions attached to a social or political cause, and except when supported by interested lobbies and governments it does not have enough money to run campaigns. In addition, activists often come under government surveillance and find it difficult to gather support by campaigning openly.

Social media helps activism in two ways: by itself becoming a medium of activism and by being an online tool for activism of the ground. In either way, social media comes handy for activists for different purposes, such as:

- Awareness and advocacy: spreading the cause and enlisting support

- Networking

- Internal communication

- Online mobilization: seeking support of netizens towards the cause

- Ground mobilization: arranging meets and protests

- Secret communication or spreading messages when the government bans regular modes of communication

- Generating social or political pressure

- Fundraising

One social media entity may not serve all purposes and types of activism; therefore, individual activists and their organizations make use of several platforms. Groups on social networking and chat platforms come in handy for internal communication; video sharing sites suit spreading visual messages to prove one's point; techniques such as hashtagging on Twitter are used for creating buzz around an issue. Activists elicit e-petitions from citizens against government decisions by using feed aggregators. When the activism is against a repressive regime, social media is very effective in bypassing bans.

In activism, as in other areas of communication, social media also supports other channels, e.g. email, phone calls, SMSs, websites, and physical sharing of messages through pamphlets and posters. When activists feel that freedom of expression is denied and disinformation is spread by authorities, they may resort to *hacktivism* or damaging the technological tools (e.g. websites, social media accounts) of such authorities or leaking sensitive information and spreading it online.

Political activists in countries with despotic rulers have been using social media for sharing wrongdoings by government officials stealthily on social media. To suppress any dissidence, many governments use strict provisions of their ICT laws, monitor social media activities and even ban them. In such cases, political opposition is known to operate through highly secure chat platforms and by opening social accounts in foreign countries.

Like activism on the ground, social media activism is not always a genuine protest against mis-governance, wrongdoings by a public authority and social ills, or in favor of positive action. Even if well-meaning, it can go out of control of its originators. It can also be a disguise for creating social ill-will and tension or destabilizing a legal and legitimate government. Sometimes political or commercial lobbies and criminals are directly or indirectly behind social media activism.

One recent example is the exploitation of farmer protest in India in 2020-21 by Canada-based Khalistan-supporters in which youth were provoked through social media (and other channels) to march to Delhi in tractors and create chaos. A tweet by noted climate activist Greta Thunberg in February 2021 exposed how well-crafted strategies are adopted for creating buzz around a topic (and that includes spreading disinformation) at the global level. The tweet, by mistake, shared the link to a document called 'toolkit' for spreading disinformation about the protest e. In the toolkit, a Khalistan terror support group chalked out a strategy to establish that serious human rights violations were being carried out by the government against the Sikh community, and the government was orchestrating a plan to take away land from poor farmers.

It has often been argued that activism on social media is a double-edged sword. The foremost concern is regarding the safety and security of activists. Social media gives a false sense of privacy to people who join movements against authorities. That makes them vulnerable to repressive action by authorities, who can use powerful technological tools to track them. In addition, propaganda agencies of rulers can generate and spread content against them. As mentioned earlier, there also are serious ethical issues associated with activism, which include social media movements being misused by vested interests and getting out of hand. This possibility is greater in the case of social media as compared to the physical world.

Another weakness of social media activism is that while the core group of activists behind a cause are a committed lot, much of activism by people at large is limited to giving quick responses on one's smartphone. Activism on social media does not test a person's commitment towards a cause, as it does not require investment of much time, energy or money in liking or sharing messages relating to that cause. It is felt that such activism, derisively called *slacktivism*, might create a false sense of massive support, and derail actual activism. It has also been noticed that even when a cause gets massive support on social media, authorities against that cause can afford to ignore it.

Yet, it cannot be denied that social media has emerged as a potent tool in the hands of common people to raise their voice collectively for social change.

A 2018 study by Pew Research Center threw up interesting insight into how people view activism on social media. 64% of Americans agreed with the statement "social media helps give a voice to under-represented groups". About 77% felt that social networking sites distract people from issues that are truly important and 71% agree with the assertion that "social media makes people believe they're making a difference when they really aren't." [ref 5]

Recent studies by the same organization found that experiences and attitudes related to political activities on social media vary by race and ethnicity, age, and party [ref 7]. Among the social issues on which US adults had changed their opinion under the influence of social media, the most important were the concern for Black lives, police brutality and racial relations – all originating from the death of a Black while being arrested for a minor offense.

Let me share some instances of effective use of social media for legitimate activism.

A series of protests against despotic and unpopular governments in the Middle East began in 2011, starting with protests in Tunisia and then spreading to Libya, Egypt, Yemen, Syria and Bahrain. Called *Arab Spring*, these protests could spread and gain mass support thanks to social media in countries with large internet penetration, e.g. Egypt. Social media usage rose tremendously in these countries and social media platforms, especially Facebook, helped significantly in organizing protests and spreading awareness. They also helped rebels in coordinating their actions.

Studies show that social media played an important role in spreading the *Occupy Wall Street* movement that started in 2011 against crony capitalism.

In New Delhi, a protest call by social activist Anna Hazare in 2011 led to massive voluntary participation by the public within hours, thanks to people telling their social media friends about their visit.

Hashtagging on Twitter is one tool that is often used by activists for spreading messages on a topic. *#BlackLivesMatter* was started in the US in 2013 to protest the acquittal of the man who had shot a black youth. It became a strong civil rights campaign and the hashtag was used by concerned people for street protests.

In 2014, *#ALSIceBucketChallenge* hashtag was started to raise charity by throwing an ice bucket on one's head and challenging friends to do so. Media reports say that in two months this hashtag had generated funds to the tune of $42 million.

Take the hashtag *#MeToo*. Started by actor Alyssa Milano to show that she too was sexually harassed the same way as others, this soon spread across the globe. Women in different spheres of activity, including churches, came out telling how they had suffered sexual harassment at the hands of influential people. In India, when it became a rage in mid-2018, many women came out with personal experiences of sexual harassment in the fields of journalism, cinema, music and politics. Even a Minister had to resign on such an allegation, some celebrities lost television/ film assignments, and the careers of some top executives were ruined.

As mentioned earlier, social media is prone to misuse, and it is easy to manipulate it with emotive messages. It was reported that some women misused the hashtag #MeToo for settling scores or seeking ransom. Fake tragic events and miseries are spread on social media to garner undeserved sympathy, collect charity or malign somebody. A case of minor mis-governance or indiscretion is sometimes blown out of proportion and made an emotional issue with a sectarian appeal to spread unrest.

USE OF SOCIAL MEDIA IN FORMAL EDUCATION

There are many apps, websites and platforms that help kids to learn different skills. There are apps for all levels of learning and skill-upgradation including on fine arts, creative writing and literature, language learning, computer coding, dance, and so on.

The use of social media as a communication tool between teachers and students is very common; many teachers and students informally share educational material, progress, projects, etc. through social media apps. In some educational institutions, students are encouraged to maintain blogs for improving their skills of expression and online socialization.

Institutions of learning, teachers and professional bodies, organizations and persons in the business of education, students and parents – all have been using social media for a range of activities.

However, the use of social media for education goes much beyond its informal use as a means of communication and as an aid to learning.

If there is one area in which blogging has contributed appreciably to the working of existing traditional institutions, it is *formal* education, especially school education covering kindergarten to 12th standard (K-12).

Edublogging

Educational blogs have been contributing appreciably to school education.

At a formal level, *edublogging* is now an established educational activity. In edublogging, tools of blogging or online publishing and engagement are used as a tool for teaching and learning in the formal educational system.

Educational blogs take many shapes and sizes. Some schools encourage blogging on free platforms. Some educational institutions have their in-house blogging ecosystem as part of their portal. Many educators/ educational entrepreneurs have opened educational portals on which they have facilities for teachers and students for various activities and provisions for interactivity and privacy. Some such portals have provisions to manage even chains of schools and universities with a number of management levels, hundreds of classrooms, thousands of teachers and a multitude of disciplines.

The following are some popular edublogging platforms:

- Edmodo [https://www.edmodo.com] is a free edublogging platform with many options for organizations, teachers and students.

- EduBlogs [https://edublogs.org] is another free edublogging platform, which offers some additional features on payment.

- Kidblog [https://kidblog.org/home] is an edublogging platform available on payment.

There are some blogs on the web, which are maintained by teachers and educationists, on which they share their subject-related expertise, educational tools and experiences of class management, problem-solving, assessment, educational policies, etc.

Many educators have shared that they find blogging useful in myriad ways such as peer-assessment, validation of formal assessment, students setting their own goals and challenging their own capabilities, collaboration, and collective problem-solving. Blogs of kindergarten and small classes, in which day's activities are showcased by teachers with the help of photographs and performance reports, let parents observe their kids' behavior and progress. School management and principals find blogs helpful in monitoring their teachers' involvement in teaching.

It has also been found that blogging can be a very effective medium for introvert children to express themselves. Interestingly, for too noisy and fitful students, blogging has been found to be a non-coercive sobering tool.

The best way to use blogs for formal education is found to be using them as a fulcrum of collaborative activities and for assessment and monitoring. While the blog itself may not be the most advanced technological tool for education, it acts as a resource center and a dashboard from which other tools and resources can be tapped.

SOCIAL MEDIA IN FORMAL RESEARCH

Though the World Wide Web is now taken seriously as a medium for publication of research papers and serious discussion on scientific and other academic topics, social media is not yet taken as serious enough for that.

On the other hand, social media has become a playground for research, especially on social, cultural, communication and health matters. A large number of papers are being written every year on the impact of social media on different human activities. Of course, social media spawns a great deal of research on information and communication technologies.

Many social media platforms have been contributing to research by funding studies on social aspects such as its impact on the young population, its usage during elections, etc.

Use of social media in crisis communication

Natural and man-made disasters and calamities are times when social media makes a great contribution but, as elsewhere, also spreads confusion and panic.

It has been observed that there is variation between the social media engagement patterns during man-made and natural disasters. During natural disasters, the flow of information usually becomes instant among people and is smooth, while during man-made disasters, the role of opinion leaders becomes important as they take conflicting positions. In disasters in which a particular group is seen to be involved or the government is seen to be not acting firmly, there is considerable distortion of information and polarization of opinions.

When Hurricane Katrina struck the American Gulf area in 2005, today's social networks had not even taken birth. People got alerts and updates mostly on radio, television and mobile phones (calls, text messages). The fast growth of social networking and instant messaging apps has completely changed communication and information exchange during disasters. Major disaster management organizations the world over try to effectively use social media in dealing with disasters.

Social media platforms are used during disaster mainly for the following purposes:

- Communication among agencies and workers dealing with the disaster before, during and after the disaster. Social media apps are the most reliable tools during most disasters. Instant messaging apps can work even with small internet bandwidth, and therefore, work even when major networks do not work during big natural disasters such as coastal hurricanes and cyclones.

- Issuing warnings, alerts, forecasts, comforting messages and updates by mitigating agencies and policing/ monitoring authorities. Such genuine and positive information helps in addressing worries and stopping misinformation. It has been seen in recent predictable natural disasters such as tropical cyclones that loss of life and property could be minimized by reaching better preparation, and constant messaging through social media had an important role in it.

- Reaching relief and rescue services to individuals in times of disaster. Since social media is available to people on their smartphones and these devices are commonplace, it is easy for rescue and relief agencies to get in touch with affected people even at an individual level. Social media is used by individuals for sending out SOS messages and requests for assistance. Social media also comes in handy in identifying survivors and victims.

- Special services by social media platforms. During major calamities, social media platforms come forward with tools for checking the safety of individuals, tracing the disaster (e.g. movement of a hurricane) on live maps, instructing people how to reach safe places, etc.

- People getting and remaining in touch with their dear ones caught in the disaster. Since social media provides many-to-many communication, it pools the resources of concerned friends and relatives and becomes the most efficient way to connect to people in the disaster zone.

- Community support. It has been seen that communities come together for help during disasters. Social media provides easy ways to organize such communities, and for other voluntary action during calamities. WhatsApp groups are quite commonly used by people for mobilizing volunteers and sharing information/ instructions with them.

- Citizen journalism and user-generated information. Especially when a disaster strikes suddenly and when it is in an inaccessible area, it is the common people at the site who spread the messages, often with photographs and videos. These help in not only alerting agencies but also providing clues and evidence that help in unraveling the cause of the disaster.

Miscreants have a field day during disasters, and social media comes in handy for creating mischief. Rumor-mongering is resorted to for creating chaos, confusing agencies and diverting resources. Panic is created and then susceptible people are exploited. Mistrust is sought to be created against authorities. Though governments, relief agencies, opinion leaders and experts try to fight misinformation, such efforts are not fully effective and social media ends up creating at least some damage.

When common people find an unusual activity in their surroundings, there is an urge to share that on social media, with conjectures about the cause or effect of that activity. This can result in the disclosure of sensitive or confidential information, as during terror attacks, anti-terror operations and military battles. Innocent miscalculation, drawing wrong inference or exaggeration of facts (e.g. 'I have myself seen a dozen bodies floating on the river.' or 'I saw the terrorists fleeing to the eastern side in a black car.') can also mislead agencies monitoring the situation or later investigating the matter.

The use of social media during the COVID-19 pandemic in 2020-21 has been discussed in detail in <u>COVID-19 and social media</u> section in <u>Impact of social media on individual lives and the society</u> chapter.

CONCERNS RELATING TO SAFETY & SECURITY, PRIVACY AND GOVERNMENT CONTROL

PRIVACY AND SECURITY CONCERNS OVER CONDUCT OF SOCIAL MEDIA PLATFORMS

Social media has proved to be a double-edged sword in different contexts: easing the life of citizens versus controlling their lives; use for public good versus use by criminals; socialization and sharing happy feelings versus leading to depression and anxiety; and so on.

Since the main segments of social media – networking, sharing and instant messaging – are platform-based, these platforms play a big role in deciding how people use them. Besides, the conduct of these platforms themselves is of paramount importance since all data and logs of people's activities reside in these platforms.

PRIVACY CONCERNS

The most important concern that the conduct of platforms creates is that the privacy of users is at risk.

Tech giants have developed mind-boggling capacities to store and process personal and private data of people connected through the internet. Social media biggies such as Facebook and Twitter can track smartphone users even though they might not be on social media. Not being on social media does not hide a person's privacy, as his friends are a big source of information about him. It is shown by experts that it is possible to create a 95% accurate profile of a person, based on his friends' accounts. In one study, experts also showed that it is possible to predict the content of a person's tweets from data of just eight of his close contacts.

These tech giants also get information through apps that do not seem to have anything to do with the collection of data. Even if you are not on Facebook, the platform can track you using various apps that use Facebook for login purposes. It was revealed in an Oxford University study of 2018 that nearly 45% of Android apps shared data with

Facebook, and the usage must have gone up by now. Kaltheuner and Weatherhead [ref 40] have demonstrated how, using development tool kits and other ways, technology providers can mine enormous data without the explicit consent of the user or with consent that was obtained through innocent-looking options. You are asked questions or given options that look obvious and innocuous but in answering them, you give up a lot of your privacy. The owner of the app or social media entity now has details of your contacts, location, camera, browsing habits, shopping preferences, and more. Even if other users may not have access to such data, the platforms themselves have it all.

The majority of apps and desktop versions of social media platforms have a feature that allows the user to decide how much of his profile and online activities can be shared and with whom. Similarly, a user can block or mute people who are obtrusive or abusive. Usually, these options are shown when the apps are installed and are available in the *'settings'* and *'profile'* sections on their account; however, most users are oblivious of such features or do not care for them.

The platforms themselves use users' profile data and data on users' browsing habits for targeting them with specific advertisements and content – all without clear consent. In addition, numerous instances have been reported when these platforms have willingly shared user data with others, and the third parties have used the data in an unethical way.

One of the most damning reports on Facebook's unauthorized sharing of users' data has been that it shared data of 50 million American Facebook users for election targeting with an election consultancy firm, *Cambridge Analytica* in 2018. Facebook responded by saying that its data was abused by a rogue researcher and it then landed with Cambridge Analytica.

In 2019, a UK parliamentary committee found that Facebook intentionally and knowingly violated both data privacy and anti-competition laws. After an 18-month investigation, it concluded that Facebook platform was being used extensively for disinformation and it was willing to sell users' data to app developers and advertisers. The Committee remarked that the internet giant was behaving like 'digital gangster' in the online world.

It was also known during investigations into the 2016 US elections that some Russian entities used Facebook, Twitter and Tumblr platforms for running disinformation campaigns before the elections – and the platforms either did not have any suspicion of such activity or chose to ignore it.

There can be a deliberate attack on people's privacy with malicious intent. Tarnishing one's competitor's image on social media is supposed to be a common phenomenon. Called *doxing*, in such privacy attacks, private information about an individual or organization/ brand is broadcast. (Of course, very rarely, private information is also made public for identifying criminals and other legal purposes.)

Even the biggest tech companies are prone to accidental or criminal breaches. Servers of all major social networks and email providers have been hacked at least once, leading to major data breaches.

Criminal breaches of data, through phishing (=impersonating a reliable person or organization to make people share data), misrepresenting genuine service providers and other ways are routine. Since users become more casual while on social media as compared to when doing monetary transactions, criminals use the social media route for entry into sensitive information. Now that many social media apps integrate in multiple ways (e.g. Facebook – Instagram – WhatsApp - mobile wallet - mobile banking), the consequences of compromise of a single app can be serious.

Privacy versus public good

Privacy and public good can sometimes go against each other. If all the content and transmission of messages are made fully encrypted and no one has access to what goes on inside a social media entity or on a web host, it would be impossible for agencies to mine it for legal and legitimate purposes. Even researchers will not be able to make use of this enormous activity/ data. Major social media platforms and web hosts/ ISPs have their own set of norms about sharing users' data with legal agencies. However, a consensus on this is yet to emerge.

Facebook CEO Mark Zuckerberg issued a note on his social media platforms (Facebook, Instagram and WhatsApp) in 2019, which seems to sum up the vulnerabilities and dilemmas of all present-day social media platforms concerning privacy: "Frankly we don't currently have a strong reputation for building privacy protective services... The future of communication will increasingly shift to private, encrypted services where people can be confident what they say to each other stays secure and their messages and content won't stick around forever... Encryption is a powerful tool for privacy, but that includes the privacy of people doing bad things... As we build our infrastructure around the world, we've chosen not to build data centers in countries that have a track record of violating human rights like privacy or freedom of expression. If we build data centers and store sensitive data in these countries, rather than just caching non-sensitive data, it could make it easier for those governments to take people's information… the best way to protect the most sensitive data is not to store it at all…" [ref 79]

In a case of private data leak from police while court proceedings were ongoing, over 3,000 pages of WhatsApp chats between a TV anchor and the head of television rating consortium in India came into the public domain in 2021. Though WhatsApp chats are encrypted end-to-end, the police seem to have accessed the chats from the smartphone of one of the individuals involved.

Privacy obligation of publishers on the web

How do social media users conduct themselves when it comes to sharing data about others? Do they behave responsibly? What are the consequences of being indiscreet in playing with others' privacy?

This subject has been discussed in detail in <u>Legal Aspects Relating to Social Media</u> chapter.

Unsafe technology

Most social media platforms have been found not doing enough for keeping users' data secure. They are lax from the very first action that a user takes: making one's profile. There is not enough scrutiny of the user's profile or his online activities, and a very large number of people with criminal intent steal others' profiles and make fake accounts. Once a person has opened a fake account on one social network, it becomes easier for him to open an account elsewhere by using his earlier account as his testimony. Similarly, with stolen identities, criminals can fool users into sharing more of their information. Social network sites are said to be focusing their eyes on traffic and money while ignoring user safety.

There have been massive leaks from the databases of many technology giants in recent years – these include Google, Facebook, Yahoo! and Fairfax.

There also have been cases when the technology giants added new features without adequate security provisions, thus risking users' personal and financial data. For example, WhatsApp, which was testing a payments app in India in 2018, was found to be not complying with the financial and identity checks for security, which were mandated by the country's central bank. The Indian government then told the company that it must locate its servers in India and strictly follow banking norms if it wanted to have a money transaction platform. One of the reasons for the closure of Google Plus in 2019 was a security compromise in the software. Facebook's *'view as'* feature that allowed users to view their own profile as someone else would, was compromised in late 2018, putting personal data of 30 million users in the hands of hackers.

One feature that has become a part of many apps is the map. In conjunction with GPS or global positioning system, it provides a large number of location-related services. From social media perspective, it can show locations in real-time, which is very useful for online and offline socialization and knowing location of people, organizations and events. However, it has serious privacy and safety implications.

Blogs can also suffer security-related issues. The two big blogging platforms, Blogger and Facebook, so far have been safe from data leaks or hacking but have had issues due to third-party codes introduced by users through widgets and plugins. Self-hosted blogs, if not adequately secured, are more prone to cyber-attacks.

Toxic content on social media platforms

All social media platforms, by their very nature, allow users to post content of their liking and are keen to have more and more content that is interesting or provocative so that the platform gets popular and gets more traffic. In this commercial pursuit, they tend to overlook their responsibility as the watchdog of the content in the platform.

IT behemoths have been pulled up by many nations' parliaments and regulatory authorities for not being responsible enough. In the last couple of years, supervisory authorities across continents have taken stringent action to discipline social media giants so that their platforms do not hurt society by spreading crime, hatred, violence and terror.

Countries across the globe want to curb inappropriate content on the web. No wonder, some of the biggest lawsuits that have been filed in the last ten years are against social media giants and in some, they have been penalized heavily.

In 2017, Germany enacted a law, Network Enforcement Act (netzDG), to put checks on social media platforms. The law stipulates heavy fines if social media platforms do not remove illegal content within 24 hours. In case the content is not so obviously illegal, they have 7 days to decide.

The fine goes up to $57 million. Some German lawmakers now want social media platforms to report messages dealing with far-right propaganda, violence, murder or rape threats, terrorist attack preparations or the sexual abuse of children to the police.

Similar laws have been introduced in France, Brazil, the US, the UK and some other countries. In Turkey an amendment to existing law to control internet, the 'social media law' has paved way for strict control on social media platforms. A bill introduced in Nepal in 2019 proposed that all social media platforms must register in that country or they could be blocked. They should also be prepared to take down content and failing to do so would invite a fine as well as imprisonment (the bill has not become law as yet). The French Constitutional Court has, however, struck down the law.

In February 2021, European Union leaders were considering legal frameworks, more than guidelines to social media platforms, which would bind these platforms to deal responsibly with user data and filter out anti-social content. A move was afoot in India in early 2021to amend the existing rules to be able to take action against social media platforms for not checking messages inciting violence.

As a consequence of pressure and threat from legislatures and authorities, social media and instant messaging platforms are forced to show that they were serious about their content and also the privacy and safety of users. In mid-2018, Twitter undertook a major exercise to clean its platform of suspicious accounts and deleted millions of accounts. Facebook claims to be cleaning out millions of toxic messages every quarter from the platform.

Twitter also claims that it regularly removes accounts associated with 'terrorist content' and has by now removed over 1.5 million such accounts. Facebook, too, has come out with similar claims.

Under severe criticism, Tumblr had to remove all its pornographic content, which was a big reason for its popularity, in one sweep in 2018.

Yet, during a shooting in a mosque in New Zealand in 2019 in which 50 people lost their lives, the live stream of shooting went viral, and social media platforms took half a day before the imagery was erased from the web. Rumors of child lifting by strangers circulated on WhatsApp for several months in India in 2018 and led to the death of 40 people before the platform took note. These are just two examples of how unprepared, and possibly casual, the tech giants have been in removing toxic content from their platforms.

After the New Zealand massacre, some countries warned social media giants to take actions for quick removal of terror content or face serious consequences including imprisonment of their top officials.

Countries are also becoming wary of social media platforms and other technology giants whose servers are not located within the country because the country's regulators cannot hold the tech entities fully accountable for their activities. Russia has blocked LinkedIn for not keeping its servers in Russia. It might block other major social networking and instant messaging platforms on the same plea. Russia and many other countries are now forcing social media platforms to install their data servers within the country. The legitimate reason for this can be to make the platforms accountable to that country's laws, but it also makes the platforms vulnerable to arm-twisting by local authorities.

INDISCRETION AND CARELESSNESS BY SOCIAL MEDIA USERS

It has been repeated many times in this Manual that social media users tend to be indiscreet and careless in choosing what they publish and spread. A big majority are also careless about the safety and security of their accounts and also their children's safety.

Copy-pasting others' content in their accounts has got many bloggers and other web publishers into trouble. Many social media users have had to face police and legal action for defamatory content.

There have been numerous cases when a small indiscretion on the part of the staff on the organization's social media account has led to their being fired. Cases of employees losing jobs and students being rusticated over nasty tweets or Facebook posts they published when emotionally upset have come in the media. Many politicians have lost their elections and many top functionaries have lost their positions after they made uncalled for comments on social platforms.

A web search throws up thousands of such examples, and they come from across the globe. Two major examples of how a single tweet caused major loss to persons in high position come to my mind and I mention them here as a reminder to social media users: Shashi Tharoor, a highly net-savvy minister in the Indian government, who had also been Under Secretary in the UN, tweeted in 2017 saying that he had traveled to his home state in 'cattle class' referring to the economy class. Considered demeaning the common flyer, the tweet raised political dust, Tharoor apologized but he had to resign. Elon Musk, the head of the iconic company Tesla, tweeted sometime in 2018 that the company was intending to go private, and taking it as a criminal intent of manipulating the company's shares, authorities slapped a whopping $20 million fine to the company. Musk also lost the chairman's post in the company.

If you want to look at the major legal provisions that directly affect social media users, please visit <u>Legal Aspects Relating to Social Media</u> chapter.

CHILD SAFETY ON SOCIAL MEDIA

I have dealt with child safety in many chapters wherever relevant. The health problems that grown-up children face due to excessive use of social media and taking it as a substitute for physical activity and real-life relationships are dealt with in detail in <u>Impact of Social Media on Individual Lives and the Society</u> chapter.

Let us, in the present chapter, discuss how children's safety can be at peril on social media and the actions parents should take to deal with it.

A quick fact-check on how children are at risk online, more so on social media:

- Children keep posting their personal details, and sometimes details about their parents, school, surroundings and life-events, which can be exploited by criminals.

- Parents themselves put their children's security and safety in danger by sharing their details, especially their photographs.

- Children's curiosity and the urge to experiment sometimes takes them to porn, gambling, drug sites.

- Poor parental supervision and guidance, coupled with peer pressure, can embolden children into taking wrong steps.

- Children often learn the tricks of dodging any supervision by parents. That gives them confidence that they can visit all types of sites.

- A false sense of confidence, especially in teenagers and young adults with a technology background, also leads many children to experiment on all types of shady websites.

- Children are prone to befriending strangers and exposing themselves online for getting more 'likes' and favorable comments than their friends.

- Schools may be careless in sharing students' data online, and school wi-fi may be insecure.

- It is easy for criminals to track a child's movement and physically harm him if GPS is enabled.

- Malicious code that is purposely entered into computers/ smartphones through software and apps, apps with permission to use personal data and other shady apps can snoop into a child's profile and exploit her.

- Criminals use many ways to harm children, e.g. phishing, befriending with the intent to harm, online bullying and threatening, offering gifts/ cash in return for a wrong action.

- Anti-social elements and fundamentalists/ terrorists use photographs and video clips to attract children into their activities and brainwash them.

- Harmful games surface now and then, in which gamers are slowly and slowly led towards some online or real crime, visit to a physical location, becoming part of a shady group or self-harm.

A criminal need not be a syndicate. Even relatives and friends with a criminal mind can harm children. Social media gives them an easy way to approach and befriend their targets.

A 2017 study by the Australian Psychological Society [ref 6] found that around 15% of teens were contacted by strangers daily, on Facebook alone. Ten percent of teens were 'actively communicating' with strangers. What is equally worrisome is that 60% of parents among the 1000 people interviewed said, they never monitored their child's social media accounts.

An Ofcom study found that between 2014 and 2019, the watching of videos on different social media platforms by children has doubled in the UK. They have also been using multiple social media platforms. Gaming has become much more popular than before among girls. Children are exposed to a lot of violent and other disturbing content including hate online [ref 50]. A survey by NCMEC on American children found that about half of the children of the 12-17 age group posted personal information online and shared it with strangers.

TikTok, the popular app that allows users to upload their videos with camera effects and music with no skills required, is reported [ref 17] to be misused by pedophiles. They have been found encouraging children to post sexually explicit videos, and children as young as 8 years are falling prey to their instructions, received mostly through comments or live-streaming.

A survey conducted by Cybermum/ McAfee on sharing of images of children by Indian parents [ref 26] found that four out of five parents in India posted photographs of their children regularly on social media, often without the child's consent. Almost all of the people surveyed agreed that the social media image could embarrass the child but posted it anyway.

McAfee has the following recommendation for parents for keeping their children safe while being online, especially on social media:

- Try to learn technology and gadgets that your kids are using or are likely to use.

- Know the risks of online presence. Before you can discuss these matters with kids, you must yourselves know the risks in using email, apps, chat and other tools for online presence.

- Discuss things out with children. Do not pontificate; do not advise on matters in which they will not value your wisdom.

- Have a supportive attitude when talking to them about such matters, especially when they are under cyber-attack or they admit to having done something wrong.

- With small kids, engage when they want to do online and even offline computer-related activities such as playing games.

- Try to understand the risks; promote activities that are interesting but safe if not educative too.

- Disable harmful apps, settings, etc. on computers, laptops and other devices. Depending upon the child's age and understanding, do this after you have discussed these aspects with the child. The least, install a malware filtering firewall and block pop-ups. Enable parental control and safety settings on the browser.

Childmind [https://childmind.org] recommends that parents must guide young ones on the use of social media on the following lines [ref 46]:

- Focus on balance: Make sure your kids are also engaging in social interaction offline, and have time for activities that help build identity and self-confidence.

- Turn off notifications: App developers are getting more and more aggressive with notifications to lure users to interrupt whatever they're doing to engage constantly with their phones. Don't let them.

- Look out for girls at higher risk of depression: Monitor girls who are going through a particularly tough time or are under unusual stress. Negative effects of social media can have more impact when confidence is down.

- Teach mindful use of social media: Encourage teenagers to be honest with themselves about how time spent on social media makes them feel, and disengage from interactions that increase stress or unhappiness.

- Model restraint and balance in your own media diet: Set an example by disengaging from media to spend quality family time together, including phone-free dinners and other activities. Kids may resist, but they'll feel the benefits.

- Phone-free time before sleep: Enforce a policy of no smartphones in the bedroom after a specific time and overnight. Use an old-fashioned alarm clock to wake up.

In a 2018 blog post, Cybermum [ref 25] has recommended that parents reverse their roles as learners and start an active conversation with children, rather than being seen as supervisors. Its specific recommendations for parents are:

- Set an example: Children learn a lot by observing their parents. So, if you don't hesitate to ask them when in doubt, they wouldn't either. Also, if parents practice digital balance, kids will usually follow suit.

- Promote mutual understanding, trust and respect: Commend your kids when they share valuable tips. Your words would act like an instant confidence booster and make them feel all grown-up and responsible.

- Extend real-life education to cover the digital one: You can establish this during your conversations about how you think real-world life-skill lessons apply to the virtual space. Talk about peer pressure, good manners, diplomacy, etiquette, etc. to drive home the point.

- Better understanding of child's digital world: Think about all that you can learn! You have first-hand knowledge of the apps they use and can later Google them to learn more about associated risks if any. You get an idea about what's trending, the new online threats and also what interests your kids and how they spend time online.

- Opportunity to test their cybersecurity awareness: Dig deep to get to know how kids secure their accounts and the content they create. Also, have a detailed chat about the merits of using licensed security tools vis-à-vis a free basic one. This lesson will last them a lifetime and ensure their online safety so spend time on this on a regular basis.

GOVERNMENT CONTROL

I have discussed in <u>Social Media Beyond Personal Socialization</u> chapter the use of social media by governments and other public organizations for spreading information and delivering citizen-services. Some aspects of government control on social media platforms for checking content have been dealt with in upper sections of the present chapter and <u>Misinformation and fake news</u> section of <u>Social Media as Mass Media and Medium of Free Expression</u> chapter. Let us discuss here how governments and their security/ investigative/ spy/ propaganda agencies handle social media for other purposes.

The main activities in this sphere include the following:

- Monitoring social media and other online activities by use of technology tools and human fact-checkers.

- Asking social media platforms to supply data on particular subjects or people.

- Asking social media platforms to block certain types of activities or particular accounts.

- Blocking social media platforms, internet or wi-fi over an area or across the nation.

- Enacting laws to give legal and policing powers in the hands of authorities, which is used for taking action against providers and users of information and communication technologies, including social media platforms and ISPs.

- Taking legal or policy decisions against particular accounts or social media platforms.

All the above actions can be done for very legitimate purposes such as checking and then tackling threats to national security, criminal activities, anti-social activities and false propaganda being spread against good work being done by the government. Since social media has the potential of being misused by criminals and other anti-social forces, governments are in fact duty-bound to monitor social media and take corrective actions.

Blocking of internet or a particular platform or a particular website/ social media account are done routinely when there is massive spread of rumors that can lead to violence and social unrest. Many countries have been restraining social media platforms against pornography, excessive violence, fake news and voter manipulations. There have also been instances when major social media platforms have been blocked or heavily fined for failing to check highly objectionable content (e.g. child pornography, terrorism) or to ensure foolproof privacy of users. Since VPN can be used for masking identity and location, some countries have banned it. Encryption of messages is how chatting apps protect their users' conversations; therefore, the Telegram app, which swears by data privacy, has been banned in many countries.

Government agencies, especially those doing investigative and espionage works, have very sophisticated and powerful tools for deep-fishing social media and monitoring conversations. They can snoop over activities of individuals and organizations by breaking firewalls and encryptions, and attacking through bots and other hidden code. These are routinely used for snooping on crime, illegal trade, terrorism and enemy activities. They can also analyze enormous data, some real-time, and use it for tracking social communications, finding out sources and broadcasters of messages, deriving social trends, etc. Much of it is an essential part of the statecraft.

On the other hand, it is common knowledge that many governments, more so the non-democratic governments, use their authority and technological tools for illegitimate purposes. Even in the seemingly legitimate areas listed above, there are grey areas prone to subjective interpretation and misuse of authority. Many governments and their agencies are known to use some or all of the following tricks for serving personal, political and financial interests of the rulers as against the public good:

- Spreading fake news and smear campaigns on social media against people, organizations or unfriendly governments.

- Maintaining a large number of fake social media accounts for trolling opponents.

- Having fake accounts for befriending on social media and then finding activities of people and their groups/ communities. Also phishing.

- Honey-trapping political targets on social, dating sites.

- Digital surveillance on individuals and their activities, for political reasons.

- Inserting malicious code and bots in messages for snooping purposes.

- Seeking private data of users from social media platforms.

- Censoring content and blocking accounts for political reasons.

- Banning or blocking specific or all social media platforms on frivolous grounds.

- Blocking internet access when not necessary from national security or law and order angles.

- Imposing tax on social media and other online activities.

- Passing draconian IT laws and using them against political adversaries.

- Mingling in other nations' affairs, such as elections, foreign relations, commerce and security.

Let us look at some recent cases of governments' actions towards control of social media. These actions range from legal and legitimate to excessive, illegitimate and illegal:

Policy analysts have been raising red-flag over covert surveillance operations by law-enforcement and investigative agencies without proper policies in place. It is argued that this leaves a wide area of discretion that is bound to be abused by the authorities. It is publicly stated by major social media platforms – Google, Facebook, Twitter - that a large number of governments approach them for getting information about accounts, removing inconvenient content and blocking accounts used for adversarial activities. Twitter has been reporting in successive years about increasing regulatory pressure from governments and 'legal threat to freedom of expression'.

WikiLeaks [https://wikileaks.org], which has exposed several cases of governments' commissions and omissions, has said that CIA had been cyber-spying by infecting computer systems at the global scale with viruses, Trojans, vulnerability-exploits and other malware. In one such case in 2017, WikiLeaks found that the several hundred million lines of code, which CIA used for this dirty hacking, had in turn been hacked from its secret vaults, with ominous portents.

In 2020-21, India blocked Chinese social media and other apps under suspicion of stealing of user data and cyber-snooping by Chinese authorities. China has denied such allegations but reports about its involvement keep appearing in the press. Similar suggestions have come up in some other countries including the US and Australia.

Many instances of foreign operators mingling in elections have been reported. Some of them have been listed in <u>Use of social media in democratic politics and elections</u> section in <u>Social Media Beyond Personal Socialization</u> chapter.

Numerous cases of blocking internet and social sites, passing repressive laws and taking unreasonably strict actions against activists have been reported from the Middle East, Central Asia, Gulf and part of Africa. Egypt, Sudan, Tunisia, Libya, Bahrain, Saudi Arabia, UAE, Turkey, Iran, Uzbekistan, Turkmenistan, … the list includes almost all nations in this area. Turkey has been imposing bans on different social media sites since the failed coup in 2016 on the pretext of national security. In 2017, Turkey blocked Wikipedia on the charge of the knowledge-sharing platform being used for a coordinated smear campaign against the nation by groups aligned with terrorists, only because the platform refused to take down four articles. Many governments the world over, including China, Iran, Turkey, Cuba, Venezuela, Myanmar, Vietnam and Pakistan, have been resorting to control of web media to quell all discussion that does not toe the line of the rulers.

Surfshark, an agency tracking the blocking of social media by governments, reported in early 2021 that out of 185 countries monitored by it, 62 had blocked or heavily restricted access to social media in past five years. [ref 68]

It is estimated that between 2010 and 2018, political parties and governments have spent more than half a billion dollars on research, development, and implementation of psychological operations and public opinion manipulation over social media.

Bloomberg has documented [ref 13] that social media manipulation and other online/ offline actions of people in power are at work in democracies and dictatorships alike in undermining people's privacy, spreading rumors and harassing uncomfortable people.

Bradshaw *et al* of Oxford University [ref 14] say, "The manipulation of public opinion over social media platforms has emerged as a critical threat to public life. Around the world, a range of government agencies and political parties are exploiting social media platforms to spread junk news and disinformation, exercise censorship and control, and undermine trust in the media, public institutions, and science. At a time when news consumption is increasingly digital, artificial intelligence, big data analytics, and "black-box" algorithms are being leveraged to challenge truth and trust: the cornerstones of our democratic society."

The Oxford University study mentioned above has also reported that social media manipulation campaigns by political parties or governments started around 2010, by 2017 at least one political party or a government agency were involved in it in 28 countries, and by 2018, this had afflicted 48 countries. Much of this growth was in countries where political parties were spreading disinformation during elections, or where government agencies felt threatened by junk news and foreign interference and were responding by developing their own computational propaganda campaigns in response. The study observed that while automation and social media teams were already in use for creating and spreading disinformation, the use of paid advertisements and search engine optimization on different platforms is on the rise.

Another global study by Oxford University [ref 15] says it has noticed *cyber troop* activity (=use of social media teams for manipulation of public opinion by governments, militaries, spy agencies, political parties, etc.) in 81 countries in 2020. It has observed that the manipulation is now pervasive and the engagement of private firms in this activity is rising. "Increasingly, states and other political actors are using social media to disrupt elections, democracy, and human rights... The strategies, tools, and techniques of social media manipulation continue to be a pervasive part of public life across all regime types. While we have identified many instances of social media manipulation used domestically during elections, they continue to be used as a tool of geopolitical influence. In 2020, for example, authoritarian countries like Russia, China and Iran capitalized on coronavirus disinformation to amplify anti-democratic narratives designed to undermine trust in health officials and government administrators," it says.

A number of countries have passed very strict laws to deal with IT, and some are said to have kept legal provisions vague that allow their abuse by authorities. Police authorities use them wantonly to book people who are inconvenient to the rulers.

A few countries have imposed taxes on online activity, including social engagement. While this appears a natural financial action by governments, and the logic often given is that social sharing and engagements and other such activities are also economic in nature as they involve connectivity, use of hardware and software, software development, data sharing, etc. Therefore, governments have a legitimate right to impose tax on online activities for bolstering their finances. In reality, such tax is usually imposed for discouraging uncomfortable social engagement.

In 2018, Ugandan and Tanzania governments imposed a tax on online social activity. The reasons given were that social media was hurting the government's developmental efforts and that the tax would be used for the nation's economic growth. The Ugandan tax is $10 a day for using social apps, and it equals the nation's per capita income! The Tanzanian law requires a registration fee of $900 a year for online publishing, thus killing almost all blogging activity. Those not abiding by the law incur a penalty of approximately $2,500 fine and are also liable to imprisonment!

Both these nations further tightened their laws to check online activity, especially social media, in the wake of elections in 2020.

In Nigeria, a bill was introduced in 2015 under which one could be jailed and fined up to $10,000 for criticism on social media. The bill was withdrawn after widespread public criticism.

Numerous cases of bloggers being wrongly booked for heinous crimes in many countries have been reported in the media. A list of such cases is available in *The Manual of Blogging* [ref 55].

Many countries have banned, for a short duration or permanently, one or more websites and social media platforms. This may be legitimate when done for tackling a real social menace or crime, but when done for a long time and indiscriminately, the underlying reason may not be as straightforward. Some countries such as Pakistan are known to be blocking social media off and on.

Russia, Iran and China have blocked Telegram nation-wide. This instant messaging app swears by end-to-end encryption of messages and is very popular in many countries. In Iran, the stated reason for blocking it is that Iran wants to promote homegrown apps to break Telegram's monopoly.

China and North Korea are extreme examples of control on social media. The Chinese government does not allow many global social media platforms to operate in China. It has its own social media platforms that are fully monitored by authorities. China filters all web content that is available to people in its territory with the help of machines and humans. The filters do not allow any information that is not liked by the Chinese Communist Party; it includes critical articles about China, the Chinese government and the Party; information about internal critics of Chinese policies; foreign content that goes against Chinese culture; discussion on Uighur Muslim activities; about 300 phrases supposed to be dangerous; and so on.

In 2015, China introduced a 'social credit' system, which rewards content that is supposed to be good by the government and imposes negative score on content perceived to be useless, wasteful or harmful. This score is used for calculating 'trustworthiness' of a citizen.

N Korea has only a small percentage of population with internet access (estimated 1% - 3%). Western and Chinese social media apps are available, but only to the elite, and with many restrictions.

Blocking and filtering the internet or a part of the web is usually done centrally in nations where the government has full control over social media, e.g. China, Vietnam, North Korea and Cuba. In other nations, blocking of sites or filtering of content is done by forcing platforms or ISPs (internet service providers) to do so in the name of threat to national security, social and religious harmony, etc. A number of technologies are available that can partially or fully disable internet/ websites/ social media across the country or in specific regions and for specific periods. Freedom House [https://freedomhouse.org], a US watchdog organization, has revealed that overall, there has been a decline in the state of freedom globally in the last 10 years till 2019, and many nations have been resorting to blocking and filtering content to suppress individual freedoms and the freedom of expression [ref 34].

SOCIAL MEDIA AND CRIME

Social media is severely criticized for helping crime, and for a good reason: it has indeed become the hotbed of criminal activities.

It is not that social media is intrinsically linked to crime but it has given new tools in the hands of criminals for (i) secret and fast communication among themselves which cannot be easily tracked by enforcement agencies, (ii) finding potential preys, (iii) spreading disinformation to create social disharmony, defame people and prompt people to commit indiscretions, and (iv) brainwashing people into crime.

Dark web (=a part of the World Wide Web, which is mostly anonymous and not searchable using normal search engines and browsers, and is, therefore, a favorite among criminals) and a number of crime-related websites and tools are already there, which are used extensively for criminal activities. Hacking, spreading malicious content, spreading self-harm games… there are numerous ways criminals continuously attack the web. What social media does is that it provides weak points, which are easy to attack. Since social media users are common people and not expert IT users, and the numbers are large, it becomes easy for criminals to exploit vulnerabilities. The probability of success is high on social media while the associated risk is low.

The vulnerabilities on social media arise mainly due to these crime-prone actions taken by platforms and users:

- Poor security architecture of the site/ platform and poor security policies.

- Poor privacy policies of the platform.

- Poor data security on the platform.

- Users not taking adequate safety and security precautions.

- Users' indiscretion in the use of social media.

As mentioned in the previous chapter, several huge data leaks have occurred in the past, making millions of user accounts prone to frauds and other crimes. In some cases, the platforms themselves have shared user data with third parties or have themselves exposed it to others.

What makes social media users especially vulnerable to crimes is their carelessness and indiscretion. Many users are ignorant about security threats online; many do not care, as they feel secure enough; many are tempted by online offers; and many want to show off their charm or assets and in doing so, they throw caution to the wind. Even the people who are cautious on other sites are seen to be careless on social media.

Whatever be their weakness – greed, gullibility, stupidity or else – users share their passwords and OTPs with others, fall to mouth-watering offers by fraudsters, share intimate pictures, chat indiscreetly, become intimate friends with strangers, share their location, post their children's pictures – and thus they themselves invite criminal attacks.

While there are individual or small-time criminal gangs that entrap social media users with baits and often get away with it, there are international criminal gangs and syndicates that use modern data mining and snooping technologies to find details about social media users. Once they have the data, criminals have a free hand.

Social media is commonly used for these major criminal purposes:

- Organized cyber-crimes. A 2019 study [ref 17] says, 'cybercriminals are earning at least $3.25bn per year from social media-enabled cybercrime, yet very little is being done to stop them.' Hacking and injecting infections into corporate or governmental systems are among their main activities.

- Converting youth into fundamentalists and terrorists. Terrorist organizations like ISIS and LeT are penetrating youth networks using online media. Once in, they share videos that show brutality against their kin, blasphemy against their religion and sermons by religious heads, for indoctrinating the members into fundamentalist ideology. Fake videos are created to brainwash youth into believing that their acts of terror have the highest religious approval and they would be rewarded enormously after their acts. Social media is used at all stages starting from offering allurements to join and showing fake clips to connecting with terror modules and communication during terror operations.

- Luring children, especially girls, into the flesh trade. Young boys and girls are easy to lure. In their unripe age, even small baits – sometimes just helping them with homework, offering chocolates in return for private information or asking them to click their own photographs for fun – can work to entrap them.

- Luring people into illicit trade and crime. The attributes of speed, secrecy and anonymity of instant messaging apps are exploited widely by criminals for high-stake economic crimes that need alertness and quick action when under threat from authorities (e.g. smuggling; trade in drugs, human organs and protected animals; money laundering). Closed groups on social media are one of the most used means of communication among criminals. Social media is also effective in keeping in touch with those who participate in crimes due to indiscretion or innocence but actually are victims (e.g. girls wanting to make an extra buck through any means, drug addicts, and habitual blood donors).

- Financial frauds. Social media suits fraudsters exceptionally well. They snoop into or hack bank accounts/ credit cards/ citizen identity details/ financial databases and get entry into linked accounts. More than that, they use social media to hoodwink, lure and threaten people to get sensitive information. People are duped by giving them allurements (e.g. quick multiplication of money), winning trust by sharing public information and then asking for sensitive information, forcing them to part with their secret information (e.g. by posing as tax authorities or bank employees; wanting to know credit card details and threatening to close the account if the information is not supplied instantly) and phishing (posing as the genuine person, organization or website), and other means.

In a major fraud committed using the networking power of social media platforms, people were duped in India, Bangladesh and other neighboring countries of their money with the promise of high returns for many years, until it was caught in 2017. People were asked to pay registration money and click some links on the website. The fraud had grown to about Rs. 37 billion and had defrauded thousands of students, salaried people and small businessmen.

- Spreading rumors and fake news. This has been discussed in detail in <u>Social Media as Mass Media and Medium of Free Expression</u> chapter.

- Bullying, trolling, blackmailing. We have discussed this in detail in <u>Impact of Social Media on Individual Lives and the Society</u> chapter.

- Destabilizing governments, etc. Recent reports on the misuse of social media by state actors (= foreign governments or their agencies) during elections and for fomenting trouble in other countries raise serious concerns about the stability of societies and democratically elected governments. For more details, you can visit <u>Concerns Relating to Safety & Security, Privacy and Government Control</u> and <u>Use of social media in democratic politics and elections</u> section in <u>Social Media Beyond Personal Socialization </u>chapter.

How social media users unwittingly become partners in crime

Mainly due to their ignorance and carelessness, and sometimes due to willingness, social media users end up committing crimes that they would perhaps not commit if they had not been indiscreet on social media. Some common such crimes are listed below.

It may be noted that creation, sharing, making comments or even storing information on one's account can make one liable to legal action, and gullibility or ignorance may not be enough defense in case the authorities or those who are harmed by such action are determined to take the social media user to task.

- Sharing and re-posting of fake news, unsubstantiated claims and fraudulent allurements received from others; rumor-mongering. While sharing may in itself not be a crime, there could be many crimes that might arise out of sharing inappropriate material.

- Indulging in chat with criminals and sharing their messages. Or, being part of groups on social media platforms in which anti-social, anti-national or fundamentalist matters are discussed and shared. Even if done innocently, this can be proved as one's association in the crime committed by those criminals.

- Exposing confidential information that may endanger others' life or property. Or, exposing identities of others, especially victims of crime and children. If such exposure hurts an individual, the responsible person cannot take the plea that he did not actually do the harm.

- Making remarks that may damage someone's reputation. The target could be a person or organization. This is regarded as defamation, and some countries have very stringent laws against it.

- Indulging in online abuse and troll. This may invite action for fanning hatred or causing mental harassment. New ICT laws have come up in many countries, with strong provisions against hateful and deliberately hurtful online activities.

- Indulging in social media trial or publicly passing judgment on an accused. This is an extension of trial by media – mainstream media proving someone guilty by deliberate negative reporting and discussion against them.

  'Trial by social media' happens to be worse than the traditional *media trial.* The person or organization under attack gets painted in black in no time on social media once one-sided stories are shared again and again. During sharing and re-sharing on social media, people add their own bias, and some even doctor photos and videos to make the story juicier. Even when no manipulation of information is done, the sheer passing of biased judgment by a large number of people has the potential to tarnish the reputation of the targeted person or organization. People indulging in this activity can be individually and collectively booked for defamation, and also for other damages to the target.

- Using others' content (e.g. photos and videos) as one's own. This can invite legal suit under copyright and patent laws. For a detailed discussion on copyright laws, you can visit <u>Legal Aspects Relating to Social Media</u> chapter.

- Editing others' content in a way that it appears out of context, and then sharing it. This is a serious offense and can invite action under laws relating to copyright/ patent, deliberately wrongful use of digital assets, forgery, etc.

LEGAL ASPECTS RELATING TO SOCIAL MEDIA

(Disclosure: I have dealt with the laws governing blogging in *The Manual of Blogging* [ref 55]. Since most of them relate to other types of social media as well, such provisions are repeated in the present book.)

Since internet came in - in the 1970s - until some years back, online activities were being dealt with in terms of the existing laws. When these old laws were found deficient, new laws started being enacted. Many countries are still in the process of enacting laws relating to ICT and the products and services arising out of them.

Online activities are developing much faster than the pace of change in the law, even in advanced and progressive nations. In nations with repressive rulers, either laws are not passed or laws are passed with the aim of controlling online activities rather than dealing with legal issues arising out of new realities.

Even when ICT-related laws are passed with the best intentions and are implemented maturely, different interpretations arise due to the nebulous nature of online activities – made fuzzier by social media. Legal cases relating to online media become especially complicated due to (i) difficulty in pin-pointing sources and finding proof of crime, (ii) sources of content/ broadcasters of content/ hosting servers/ headquarters of platforms being situated outside the country concerned, (iii) lack of clarity about the accountability of platforms about the content, (iv) thousands of lay users becoming partners in crime due to indiscretion but no criminal intent, (v) low level of international legal and policing cooperation, and (vi) conflict of interests among governments due to political reasons, and perceived or real conflicting national interests.

Sometimes the implications of actions as well as court orders are serious as they relate to suppression of freedom of expression, breach of privacy of a large number of users, the spread of malicious content from outside the jurisdiction of a country, etc. Implementation of court orders also becomes difficult in case of cross-country crimes or when orders affect a large community.

At the same time, numerous petitions with trivial, sometimes absurd, charges flood courts. In the US, courts' time is being spent on cases relating to questions such as whether the President or a government official can block a user on his social media account, and whether the President can delete his own tweets.

The web, especially social media, is wantonly used for all types of nefarious activities. Freedom of expression is taken too far, with no respect for others' reputation and privacy. Though social networking and instant messaging platforms try (at least they claim to be trying) to check such activities, criminals and other anti-social individuals and groups seem to have an upper hand.

There is another important dimension: abuse and misuse of legal and administrative power in the hands of authorities. I have dealt with this aspect, with examples, in <u>Concerns Relating to Safety & Security, Privacy and Government Control</u> chapter.

In this complex play of a range of crimes on one hand and laws, their interpretation and enforcement on the other, social media users are often drawn unwittingly into embarrassing or legal situations. Individual social media users who write or comment strongly on political, security and social issues are much more likely to suffer because unlike mainstream journalists, most of them have not studied laws that directly or indirectly govern freedom of expression and they do not have the backing of media houses, trade bodies and professional associations.

Most users are found to be casual in their approach towards legal considerations. The perceived veil of distance and anonymity makes them bold and reckless, and they publicly air hatred and extreme opinions, which they would not otherwise do. The sentimental ones make political and social comments without thinking much, and often fight with those having opposite views. More adventurous and more socially or politically active bloggers and commenters open chat groups and fake social accounts to promote their views and berate others. No wonder, they invite action from governments, opponents and criminals.

Social media users who use the medium purely for personal socialization usually write safe and harmless content. But they copy-paste passages, photos and videos at will. A majority of them seem to think that whatever information is available on the web can be re-used. Even if they are conscious of 'stealing' the content, they might do so thinking that the owner of the copied matter would never know about it or would not bother to take action against them.

Even a very genuine use of something that by common sense is not likely to be claimed by someone as his property may cause problems for people using that content without permission. An extreme example of this is the case of 'monkey selfie'. It so happened that wildlife photographer David Slater left his equipment in an Indonesian forest in shooting condition and a macaque monkey pressed the click button, thus taking his selfie. He was sued by the animal rights group, PETA, in 2015 claiming that the selfie belonged to the monkey and Slater had infringed his copyright by publishing the photograph as his own. Impoverished after a two-year long legal battle, Slater finally managed to reach a compromise in 2017.

Traditional bloggers are likely to be more vulnerable for their actions as compared to casual commenters on social networking sites because bloggers are much more strongly identified with their content and views. They also are noticed by criminals and governments alike as their blogs have an identity more distinct than an account on a social networking platform.

Cases of bloggers being booked come to light now and then but a significant volume of case law has not yet taken shape. A large number of bloggers in many countries have been arrested by authorities, sometimes with politically motivated use of law or administrative powers. A number of social media publishers ('bloggers' in general parlance) have faced defamation, copyright infringement and plagiarism.

IMPORTANT LAWS THAT DIRECTLY RELATE TO SOCIAL MEDIA USERS

Social media users should be aware of their rights and limitations in the following areas, and keep themselves abreast of the concerned laws:

Freedom of expression

All nations have their own laws on freedom of expression. At one end of the spectrum, in some countries, the freedom is guaranteed by the constitution and on the other end – in most countries ruled by kings, military rulers or a single party - the freedom barely exists. As such, the related laws may give liberty to people to express political and social (including religious) opinions freely or may be highly restrictive. Users of social media must express themselves within the limits available in their countries or be prepared to face legal consequences.

It is globally accepted that the freedom to express cannot be wanton and must adhere to universal norms, and that governments can impose *reasonable restrictions* on the freedom of expression. Even in most liberal societies, some types of expression are not allowed. At the minimum, one must not indulge in creating or sharing content that is libelous, meant to incite hatred or violence, in highly bad taste (e.g. showing gory violence), and universally accepted as inappropriate (e.g. child pornography and terrorism).

Intellectual property rights

Every nation has one or more laws for the protection of copyright of the creator of original work and protection of trade rights and inventions. Thus, works in any format, e.g. text, image, audio or audio-visual, are protected by these laws as also performing arts, research reports, patents and trademarks.

As a rule, social media users must not copy others' content without the creator's/ copyright owner's permission, except when the use of the material is allowed without permission. Stealing of content becomes even more serious when it is used for commercial or research purposes.

There are some situations in which use of such material is freely allowed, e.g. a small portion of a book or report for citation or critique; generic details of a public event taken out of published reports; material that is '*in public domain*' due to very old age or other reasons; material that has been allowed to be used according to '*Creative Commons*' terms; and material on which the creator has voluntarily given up copyright. Creative Commons [https://creativecommons.org] is a non-profit organization based in the US. It has a set of copyright certificates that people can apply to their creative works.

Social media users are often under the misconception that they can edit text taken from others' blogs/ websites/ printed works and use it on their social media accounts. Many also assume that images, audio and video available freely on the web can be shared on their accounts. The fact is that copy-pasting from others is considered a serious crime and if the creator of that work is determined to take the copy-paster to court, there could be serious trouble for the unauthorized user. In some countries, people are very sensitive and un-pardoning when copyright is violated. Many bloggers and website owners have faced legal trials on this count.

The copyright regime may see a further tightening in the future, with European Union paving the way. In 2018, the EU came out with its *Copyright Directive*. Two of its articles are worth mentioning, as these will shape the way content is handled by tech giants in the years to come. Article 11 of the Directive makes news aggregators pay media companies a 'link tax' when sharing their content. Article 13 demands that platforms filter out intellectual property violations before publishing any content, by using automated software.

Attribution and disclosure

Whether permission for use of content is required or not, it is expected that whenever another person's or organization's content is used, it is duly acknowledged. Though sharing routine information and forwarding images and videos may not need such attribution, users must attribute the source when something of significance is used. That applies especially to quotes, arts and paintings, and research.

Similarly, it is necessary that whenever social media users/ influencers recommend or endorse a product, service or brand, they should disclose their commercial dealings with that entity. This should be followed scrupulously when the recommendation or endorsement is of a definitive (not casual) nature, e.g. product reviews on a blog. When there is a commercial consideration behind a recommendation, the same must be disclosed. For example, when a blogger or social influencer receives a book or beauty product free for review, or is given a free stay in a hotel for writing a favorable article, he must disclose that in the review/ article itself. Like other legal provisions, different countries have their own laws on this; the 'guides' issued by the Federal Trade Commission (FTC) of the USA [https://www.ftc.gov] offer very comprehensive guidance on this matter.

Privacy rights

Another very important set of laws that social media users can confront is those relating to an individual's *privacy*. In general, a social media user is liable if he has written or shown something that is considered private. Courts have come down heavily on bloggers in some countries for publishing private content. Infringement of privacy is usually allowed only when it can be proved that the interest of the society is served by exposing private information about a person (or a firm).

With the promulgation of General Data Protection Regulations (GDPR) by the European Union in 2018, all web publishers and others who capture personal data of visitors must conform to some basic norms for proactive declarations and data storage, usage and sharing. Though applicable legally within the EU region, it has found wide international acceptance. Under these regulations, any social media platform, individual blogger or website owner cannot collect visitors' information without their consent. It has high relevance to blogging because as a publisher, the blogger does capture visitors' personal data (e.g. name, email ID, location, and browsing preferences) knowingly or unknowingly (through cookies stored on web browsers). When such information is collected for e-commerce, email marketing or other purposes, it must be kept safe and not be shared with third-parties without permission of the person concerned.

Defamation and libel

When someone makes a false statement that tarnishes another person's reputation or shows him in poor light, he can be charged with *defamation* or *libel* (= defamation in writing). A person can be held guilty of defamation even if his act is due to negligence or ignorance and not with malice. Only in the case of criticism of public figures, he (the public figure) is required to prove malice.

Some social media users copy juicy news items, images and videos from the web and publish them on their blogs and social media accounts, without a sense of responsibility. People morph others' images and videos either for fun/ parody or to deliberately damage someone's reputation, and this has become a child's play with media-editing apps. Now that deep-faking video apps have become common, one can easily replace one person with some other even on videos. Sometimes videos showing products of a brand in poor light come up on social networks and chat platforms. If proved to be spreading falsehood about a person or a brand, the creator of such content has no protection of law on the excuse that he did not intend to damage a person's/ brand's reputation. Similarly, the one who shares such content has no defense on the ground that he only forwarded the content received from someone else. Courts can be very unforgiving in the case of defamation.

Criminal laws

There are many other legal provisions that the social media user is directly subject to. These include laws relating to the propagation of adult material, honoring national symbols, minority rights, and so on. Investigation agencies and courts may establish complicity of the social media user if the material published on his blog/ social media account leads to the commitment of a crime.

Governments can invoke special laws at the time of riots, emergencies and war. Election laws in some countries strictly prohibit *'paid news'* in which a paid article is written in favor of a candidate or a political party in the garb of a news piece.

Disclosing the identity of a rape victim or child victim is not only deeply unethical, it is also a specific crime in many countries.

IMPACT OF SOCIAL MEDIA ON INDIVIDUAL LIVES AND THE SOCIETY

THE SOCIOLOGY OF SOCIAL MEDIA

Social media and its main carrier, the smartphone, have become part of our lives. People are often seen to be paying more attention to their smartphone when they are having a family dinner or a function where they are expected to pay undivided attention to friends, family and guests. A number of cases have been reported in the media of onlookers recording videos rather than saving a girl from goons or helping a person hit by a vehicle. Cases of persons being hit while crossing a busy road with their eyes glued to the smartphone are carried by the press now and then. When on a nature trip, people seem to be more interested in getting an impressive selfie fit for their Facebook or Instagram account rather than enjoying nature's beauty. Later on too, we are not interested in looking at the photograph to re-live the beauty of the surroundings but in finding how many people have liked it or made appreciative comments on our social media account where we shared it.

Our obsession does not stop at seeking appreciation, we also are keen to find out who among our friends did not make a salutary comment on the photo, and we hold a grudge against them.

It has been observed that people's preference for different types of social media and different platforms depends on age, gender, educational level, even nationality. Blogging for socialization no longer attracts the younger generation. Facebook too seems to be losing ground among young people in favor of more visual and local networks and instant messaging platforms. Women are found to be in higher numbers than men on Instagram. As you would intuitively expect, a Pew Research study of 2018 affirmed that as the age grows, the use of social media in the US population goes down. The younger lot (18-29 years) prefer YouTube, Facebook, Snapchat and Instagram over Twitter. Pinterest is much more popular among women than men. LinkedIn is popular among graduates and those from high-income households. Though most users are active on an average on three social media platforms and most users visit their favorite social media sites daily, over half of Americans said, they would not find it hard to give up social media if required [ref 62]. (Looking from the other side of the coin, about half would not be able to give up social media!)

There also are studies that suggest the plateauing of social media use in advanced countries. To quote one, Edison Research [ref 31] has found that Facebook had lost 15 million users in the US in 2017-18, particularly teens and young adults. If they have flocked to Instagram, an app from the same stable, Facebook as a company does not lose much; it is gain for a younger, more visual and simpler platform. COVID-19 has, however, given new propulsion to the main social media platform, and it is believed that this would wane over time.

In the last 4-5 years, short-video apps such as TikTok have become highly popular in many regions of the world, aided by fast penetration of smartphones in the country-side and data getting cheaper.

Does social media make people happy?

It is no brainer that social media helps people in many ways, e.g. receiving information/ news and knowledge, finding answers to problems and getting entertainment. Many such attainments through social media keep people happy. There are some studies available on the WWW, which indicate that, overall, social media has a positive impact on people.

In a study of Facebook, Ozimek *et al* [ref 52] concluded that the platform has a positive impact on users' emotions because they use it for satisfying their materialistic goals. Depending on their mental state, they use it for affirming their qualities, feeling better or accumulating materialistic possessions. In another study, Dibb [ref 28] found that users compare their physical health with others on Facebook, which also has positive consequences (in addition to some negative consequences).

A 2018 study among US teens by Pew Research Center [ref 4] found that about 81% of them feel "that social media makes them feel more connected to what's going on in their friends' lives, while around two-thirds say, these platforms make them feel as if they have people who will support them through tough times. And by relatively substantial margins, teens tend to associate their social media use with positive rather than negative emotions, such as feeling included rather than excluded (71% vs. 25%) or feeling confident rather than insecure (69% vs. 26%)."

Social media impacts well being

Social media does create problems of many types – physical health, emotional health, social disengagement, accidents… Some of these have been discussed in <u>Concerns Relating to Safety & Security, Privacy and Government Control</u> and <u>Social Media and Crime</u> chapters. We will discuss physical and emotional health issues in the next section.

Social media when someone does not want it

All platform-based social media accounts can be closed at will, and blogs, of course, can be made private or deleted. Many social media platforms also give privacy options to customize the way one is seen on the web.

However, it has been found through studies that traces of one's social media life remain even after one has ceased to exist on the social media. The main reason for this is that the account has not been fully deleted. The other big reason is that the content has been shared on different web-spaces. The web content is also routinely stored by search engines, web archivers, trackers, directory compilers, aggregators, etc.

The other issue with plugging off of social media is that life may become difficult, at least for some, without the apps that become part of their lives. The difficulty could be real or imaginary. The real problems could be not being able to connect in times of need or to use features of the app for paying bills, managing health parameters, etc. The impact of social media vacuum can also manifest in mental health issues and 'withdrawal symptoms' when one does not get updates, appreciation or sweet-nothings from friends, or is unable to show oneself off. If one quits social media after hours of usage every day, and does not pick up something useful to fill the time hitherto being spent on social media, that can result in falling into an unwanted and wasteful activity. Those afflicted with *social media addiction* can face more serious symptoms if they suddenly switch off social media.

Social media after one's death

When people die, their social media accounts and the content in them remain alive. That can have undesirable consequences for their descendants, friends, etc. On the other hand, some family members might like the accounts of their dead loved ones to live on as their memories. In some cases, especially when the accounts are not in personal names, people could like to continue the accounts and associated activities.

The number of dead people's accounts on social media platforms runs in millions. On Facebook alone, about 3.5 million users die in a year.

Major platforms have made policies regarding how the account of the deceased is to be operated/ closed. For example, Twitter is amenable to working with an immediate family member to deactivate the account, but the platform does not hand over the account to anybody. Facebook gives its users the option of having their account permanently deleted after their death or to give a legacy contact (=contact who can use the account after one's death).

Social media influences opinions

It was the initial common notion that social media makes noise without actually influencing people because it does not purvey serious content and people do not trust it anyway. But many surveys and studies have established that it does influence people's opinions, sometimes in significant ways.

Children and those exposed to social media suddenly (without first being exposed to other online activities such as emailing) are more likely to trust messages on social media. Even grown-ups and mature social media users tend to trust and get influenced by the content they receive on social media, especially when the content looks genuine, and comes from friends, experts and official channels.

This study by Pew Research [ref 56] is worth a detailed mention: In a 2020 survey, the research agency asked US adults about four different types of activities that they may have engaged in on social media platforms. 36 percent of them said they had used sites like Facebook, Twitter and others in the past month to post a picture to show their support for a cause; 35% said they looked up information about rallies or protests happening in their area; 32% used it to encourage others to take action on issues they regarded as important. A smaller share (18%) reported using a hashtag related to a political or social issue on social media during this time. 23% of social media users said they had changed their views about a political or social issue because of something they saw on social media in the past year.

Notable differences were found according to race, ethnicity and age. Asian American, Black and Hispanic social media users were more likely than their White counterparts to say they have changed their views on a political or social issue.

The survey also found that social media seems to be making a bigger impact on people as compared to earlier. in 2020, 76% of social media had not changed their views on a political or social issue because of something they saw on social media in the past year, as compared to 84% in 2018.

Sophisticated tech tools and psychological concepts are employed to influence public opinion during elections. Governments themselves are supposed to be playing mind-games with their citizens on social media. The use of social media to influence people by foreign governments not favorably inclined towards a country or a political formation is now commonplace. The influence of messages from celebrities and close circles seems to be more pronounced now, because of social media. Most people are bound to change their opinions under so many influences, albeit to different degrees. I have discussed these influences in much greater details in <u>Misinformation and fake news</u> section of <u>Social Media as Mass Media and Medium of Free Expression</u> chapter, <u>Concerns Relating to Safety & Security, Privacy and Government Control</u> chapter and COVID-19 and social media section of <u>Impact of Social Media on Individual Lives and the Society</u> chapter.

PHYSICAL & MENTAL HEALTH ISSUES ASSOCIATED WITH SOCIAL MEDIA

The effect of social media on human health has been studied by many research organizations, and in fact, the study of *social media and mental health* is emerging as a new area of research and health practices.

Studies have established that children and young adults are the most affected. Teens tend to have issues relating to fitting in the peer group, and these are accentuated by social media because they need to constantly come to the expectations of their friends and also show off their assets including beauty/ handsomeness, wit/ intelligence and mastery of social media tools. Since on social media, users tend to post their positive experiences and hide the negative ones, everybody tries to excel others in showing oneself off, leading to a sort of vicious cycle of show-off – show off by others - feeling of self-doubt – more show off.

The high prevalence of social media in the lives of teens and young adults is argued to be causing depression because their socialization through social media is less empathic and deep as compared to socialization at a physical level. For this reason, teenagers who also maintain an offline social life tend to be less affected than the ones addicted to social media.

Some studies have concluded that social media use causes depression, especially among teens. Girls are reported to be affected more than boys. In one US study, it was found that the use of more social media platforms leads to increased levels of depression and anxiety irrespective of the overall time spent on social media [ref 57].

A study found a statistically significant correlation between social media use and depressive symptoms in young people: young people who used social media excessively were found to be more likely to face depression. Another research confirmed a link between social media use and social isolation among American young people [ref 69].

Some studies have revealed a widespread rise in eating disorders among girls due to their trying to look skinny like the ones whose pictures they constantly see on social media.

Among many available on the web, this 2018 research [ref 43] affirms a close linkage between the use of highly visual social media (Instagram, Snapchat) and body image concerns among girls, which may lead to poor psychological adjustment. Girls are reported to develop symptoms of low self-esteem and anxiety when they compare themselves with others' images on visual social media platforms. The image-enhancing features on such platforms make a selfie look much more charming than the subject in real life, and regular users of these platforms tend to compete with others in looking more beautiful.

It has also been observed that people with criminal minds purposely induce young girls to self-harm and suicidal behavior.

Excessive use of social media leads to sleep disorders and sleep deprivation that in turn lead to many physical and mental health issues. The major primary reasons for social media led sleep-related issues are: sleeping for less time, going to bed late, change in biological rhythm and effect of screen light on eyes [ref 48].

Heavy use of social media is also linked to the youth not spending enough time on physical exercises and sports.

In a 2018 study of British young people (aged 14 to 24 years) by the Royal Society for Public Health (RSPH), young people and youth said Instagram was the most negative among five popular social media platforms [YouTube, Twitter, Facebook, Snapchat and Instagram] in terms of mental health and well-being [ref 78].

It has been established empirically that the interplay of many disorders can lead to serious mental health issues [ref 41].

Once in a while, harmful addictive games/ challenges are introduced on the web with criminal intent. The computer game *Blue Whale* led to many deaths of young people in many countries between 2016 and 2018. Started in Russia in 2013, the game guided gamers into committing suicide in the final stage of the game. There are hundreds of games available online and for download that pose a serious threat to the emotional well-being of youth. Some of these have been banned in many countries but can be easily accessed by use of peer-to-peer file-sharing networks and other methods.

Social media is also found to be addictive, much like psychoactive drugs such as cocaine and dopamine. Though only a small percentage of social media users fall into addiction, the number could range between 5 and 10 percent in highly connected societies. AddictionCenter [ref 83] has this to say about social media addiction (formatting by me): "Addictive social media use will look much like that of any other substance use disorder, including

- mood modification (i.e., engagement in social media leads to a favorable change in emotional states),

- salience (i.e., behavioral, cognitive, and emotional preoccupation with social media),

- tolerance (i.e., ever-increasing use of social media over time),

- withdrawal symptoms (i.e., experiencing unpleasant physical and emotional symptoms when social media use is restricted or stopped),

- conflict (i.e., interpersonal problems ensue because of social media usage), and

- relapse (i.e., addicted individuals quickly revert to their excessive social media usage after an abstinence period).

Online abuse

One common emotional attack on people with gender, race and geographical identities through social media is through trolling and the use of abusive language. Ruthless comments are passed to provoke people and make them emotionally unstable.

According to Amnesty International [https://www.amnesty.org], a woman is abused on Twitter every 30 seconds. In 2018, Amnesty International came out with a report, *#ToxicTwitter* [ref 2] that showed that women faced all sorts of undignified treatment on Twitter. It was reported that women faced harassment on all social media platforms but Twitter made it worse because of sheer numbers.

Towards the end of 2018, another study by Amnesty, called *Troll Patrol*, re-affirmed that situation in the US. "We now have the data to back up what women have long been telling us: Twitter is a place where racism, misogyny & homophobia are allowed to flourish, basically unchecked," Amnesty tweeted in December 2018. Its key findings of the project Troll Patrol are worth sharing:

- Black women were disproportionately targeted, being 84% more likely than white women to be mentioned in abusive or problematic tweets. One in ten tweets mentioning black women was abusive or problematic, compared to one in fifteen for white women.

- 7.1% of tweets sent to the women in the study were problematic or abusive. This amounts to 1.1 million tweets mentioning 778 women across the year, or one every 30 seconds.

- Women of color (black, Asian, Latin and mixed-race women) were 34% more likely to be mentioned in abusive or problematic tweets than white women.

- Online abuse against women cuts across the political spectrum. Politicians and journalists faced similar levels of online abuse and we observed both liberals and conservatives alike, as well as left and right-leaning media organizations, were affected.

Many surveys have found that young people routinely face trolling, cyber-bullying and other forms of online harassment on social media.

A survey by Pew Research Center [ref 4] found that in 2018, over 59% of US teens had faced some form of harassment on the web. Offensive name-calling was found to be the most common form of cyber-bullying. Teens also saw the spread of rumors about them, received explicit images that they had not asked for, were asked questions again and again about their address and activities, got physical threats and saw their explicit images shared on social media without their consent.

COVID-19 AND SOCIAL MEDIA

COVID-19, the disease caused by a form of flu virus – SARS coronavirus (technical name: SARS-CoV-2), started in December 2019 from the

Chinese city of Wuhan and soon turned into a pandemic of a scale never seen before. The first such event after the advent of social media, it led to the use and misuse of this medium in significant ways.

Since the bare facts about the pandemic will be forgotten in future, let me give a couple of paragraphs on the pandemic so that the dates and facts given later in the chapter are understood in proper context.

In December 2019, Chinese authorities and in January 2020 WHO declared that a new form of coronavirus had spread in Wuhan province. Soon, reports of its spread started coming from Japan, South Korea, the US, European nations and other parts of the world. By end-March 2020, it had spread to the entire world, killing about 3,000 people a day. Only a few secluded regions of the world remained untouched.

Some existing treatments were tried and, as they failed, new ones were recommended by national and global authorities. No sure-shot treatment could be found and vaccine remained the only hope to fight the disease. Wearing of masks, regular washing of hands and social distancing were found to be the best preventive measures. National and provincial authorities tried all possible measures to check the spread of the disease, including lockdowns. These hurt economies and people badly, and some sectors of economy and small businesses crashed. Unemployment rose and pay cuts happened on a large scale. Countries came out with stimulus packages, employers allowed work-from-home. To the extent possible, hitherto offline activities were carried out online.

By the end of the year, the virus had infected over 100 million people and caused 2.15 million deaths. The world economy had gone under recession.

As early as January 2020, the virus was successfully grown in the lab and its genetic sequencing started. The race to come up with vaccines started in February 2020. Since time was of great essence, new technologies coupled with new international protocols were put in motion to accelerate vaccine development. International cooperation and funding helped, and vaccines started rolling out for public use in the last months of 2020. Some countries and regions that had earlier started seeing a decline in infection witnessed new waves of COVID-19 in late-2020 and in 2021.

Actions taken by major social media and other tech platforms during COVID-19

From the very beginning, top tech companies were alive to the role online media would play if the coronavirus became a pandemic. It did not take much time before that happened, and the companies started being criticized for not doing enough. So, in March 2020, Microsoft, Facebook, Google, LinkedIn, Reddit, Twitter and YouTube came out with a joint statement: "We are working closely together on COVID-19 response efforts. We're helping millions of people stay connected while also jointly combating fraud and misinformation about the virus, elevating authoritative content on our platforms, and sharing critical updates in coordination with government healthcare agencies around the world. We invite other companies to join us as we work to keep our communities healthy and safe..."

Tech giants, including those having social media, search, cloud hosting and email platforms, collaborated with the WHO and national authorities in different ways. Some of them created websites and trackers devoted to the pandemic, and used tech tools to see that their platforms do not become tools for the spread of misinformation. Most of them provided donations and support in dealing with the pandemic as well as the infodemic (=epidemic of information =excess of information, especially misinformation).

COVID-19 tested the content policies and enforcement systems of the big social media platforms, especially Facebook and Twitter, as they were among the most used platforms for information exchange during the pandemic and came under harsh public scrutiny. However, though it is public knowledge that instant messaging platforms such as WhatsApp and Telegram played a bigger role in spreading inappropriate content, they got to escape in the name of privacy. End-to-end encryption of their messages also ensured that researchers and watchdogs did not get data on the abuse of their platforms.

Social media platforms, including Facebook, YouTube, Instagram, Twitter, WhatsApp and Telegram, claim to have customized their machine tools for giving better visibility to authentic sources of information when people searched for information or advisories about the disease. They also promoted correct information by the use of hashtags and by promoting correct information when people tried to trend hashtags. Their community tools and features (e.g. groups, channels) also came in handy for creating useful information and advisories on the pandemic. Besides giving the choice to users to flag or block inappropriate content, some platforms also provided a mechanism to report this to the platform.

Facebook says [ref 39], it acted responsibly and proactively all through the COVID-19 period by collaborating with authentic agencies in the spread of health communication, promoting supportive communication, and removing misinformation from the platform. It also financially supported fact-checkers and health and economic relief efforts, including mental health.

Facebook hs also claimed to be banning ads that promote merchandise to exploit the COVID-19 situation and banned ads that discouraged people from getting vaccinated. However, skeptics blame the platform for not doing enough to remove toxic content and continuing with surrogate ads.

Twitter proactively started some of its own Twitter accounts and hashtags to spread correct background information, advice and updates on COVID-19.

Twitter has stated that it used machine tools as well as a constant human review to clean its systems like never before. In early 2020, Twitter broadened its definition of 'harm' so as to make its intentions clear about removing misleading and harmful content relating to the pandemic. It increased its capacities and collaborated with other organizations to flag or remove content that did not pass muster.

Twitter had to remove tweets of Brazilian President Jair Bolsonaro that went against the science-based facts and advice on the disease. The platform received flak from the public when initially it did not act decisively on such tweets from US President Donald Trump, but it did start flagging his indiscreet tweets subsequently.

Among other specific actions by social media platforms, WhatsApp reduced the number of times people could forward messages; Telegram came up with stickers in support of health workers, social distancing, etc.; Instagram came up with stay-home stickers; Facebook Messenger came out with free developer tools for government agencies; YouTube screened out many videos promoting self-treatment of the disease; Sapchat introduced bitmoji stickers with advisories. Some platforms hosted livestreams, hackathons, quizzes, etc. to involve audiences in COVID-19 related actions.

Institutional initiatives and social media

As far as dealing with information, most institutions (including national and local governments, health agencies, essential service providers, media and social media watchdogs, global organizations, scientific and research organizations and educational institutions) were overwhelmed from the very beginning. They had to spread messages about their own work and steps they were taking to tackle the situation, communicate with stressed employees, and counter misinformation in general and about themselves. Except for a few, they did not have experience and institutional memory of having handled such a situation.

While other organizations and agencies had a small area to cover, national governments had an extremely daunting challenge, especially in times when the pandemic was going out of hand.

Let's come to the specific task of dealing with information. In earlier days, it would have been easy for governments and institutions to channel information through press briefings and take the traditional media by their side, but social media changed all the rules of the game. It was a channel that had the potential to carry a positive message far and wide and also spread negativity almost in real-time.

Government/ public agencies usually suffer from a trust deficit, and some sections are especially suspicious when they consider the government or the party not favorably inclined towards them. In such cases, social media becomes a playground for spreading anti-government sentiment, more so when opinion leaders join the fray. For example, in some racial and religious sections in many countries, social media played a big role in creating and spreading vaccine hesitancy.

Healthcare professionals generally had a high trust value across sections. In one study, though nearly half the users said they depended on social media for news, only a third considered it reliable. However, news coming from health experts/ organizations was felt to be more reliable. [ref 70] Some governments did a good job of putting health organizations and experts in the forefront of their COVID-19 communication, but many other governments used traditional 'spokespersons' and thus failed to carry the public opinion with them. In the US, President Trump took it to the extreme, trashing scientific opinion and side-stepping his top health experts. Most of the time, social media reinforced his views and made people harden their own views on political lines on subjects ranging from the origin of the disease to available treatments, need for quarantine and social distancing, vaccination, etc..

Some governments used celebrities and other influencers for engaging on social media. It was seen that as against their informal personal messages on social media, the messages that got broadcast by public agencies from celebrities were formal and technical. For example, film and sports personalities explaining the health benefits of social distancing and cleanliness. This type of messaging might not have brought about the desired behavior change towards social distancing, etc.

A good amount of coordination between government agencies and social media platforms was seen almost across the globe. That helped in spreading the right information and fact-checking of suspicious information, news and advisories being spread on social media. Social media did a splendid job in spreading 'protocols' evolved by the WHO, health authorities and governments about treatment, personal protection equipment, movement in public places, management of resources, and vaccination.

Scientific communication got a boost during COVID-19. Social media helped research journals and scientists in the field of healthcare explain research to people without the need for intermediation by traditional media. Seeing the demand for first-hand scientific information, some research institutes and publications came out with resource pages devoted to COVID-19 related research. Among the most active major scientific institutes and journals, one can name The Lancet, Nature and Johns Hopkins University.

In some cases, health professionals erred in responding in the face of their urge to get popular on traditional and social media or due to sheer inexperience. There were many instances all along when health authorities came out supporting an untested treatment and trashing some other. Some started advising treatments based on unfounded but seemingly sound logic. Scientific journals and researchers also kept on sharing their preliminary findings, which were immediately lapped up by social media and presented as absolute truth, leading to confusion, worries and wrong treatment.

It was also seen that even the best responses from government bodies were common-sensical rather than supported with psychological and behavioral tools, though a lot of research is available and could have been useful. Perhaps a big opportunity to use such insights on social media was wasted, people were not sensitized enough to follow social distancing and other preventive guidelines, and lives were lost.

Another opportunity provided by social media, which was not used properly by public agencies at large, was making use of instant feedback that comes on social media. A look at the social media response of some major governments during the COVID-19 period shows that more emphasis was on disseminating facts and figures and trying to convince that the government was doing its best and its efforts were making an impact. A better way, which has been witnessed during natural calamities, of responding to worries, needs and misconceptions being shared on social media, was missing.

Teaching institutes and students were also badly affected due to the pandemic and in many ways. Teachers had a tough time teaching online, ensuring online attendance, checking homework, etc. More than institutional arrangements by universities and schools, what played a major role in supporting remote learning were video-sharing and streaming apps, social media and pre-recorded lectures provided by top-level public agencies. WhatsApp groups were very useful for group communication and collaboration.

Consumption of social media during the pandemic

As described above, COVID-19 changed the way individuals, families, schools, societies, markets, small and big firms, utility agencies, offices and governments functioned. It forced people inside their homes - some away from home and some forced to share the same space they were not used to. Many people, especially children and aged people faced serious mental-health issues as they were not able to cope with the situation.

In this changed lifestyle, consumption of digital data for personal communication increased in all geographies and among all social groups. Gaming also saw a big jump, and its use on social media platforms increased manifold.

While socialization and entertainment on social media met people's emotional needs, social media fulfilled their need for information and satisfied their curiosity and urge to remain updated. It is reported that social media was often much faster than the traditional media in bringing alerts and sensing the looming developments. Look at this observation by Das and Ahmed [ref 27]: "…our preliminary research shows that the spread of the virus across Italy became apparent significantly earlier, on social media than in the mainstream media. A looming stock market crash and global economic crisis are also apparent from the sentiments around trending Twitter topics such as — #BlackMonday and #StockMarketCrash2020 – long before they were reported in traditional outlets."

As was expected, video communication over the internet increased, be it sharing of videos on traditional vlogging platforms (e.g. YouTube), fast adoption of shot-video sharing platforms (e.g. TikTok), OTT (over the top: video streaming and shows online as compared to television, e.g. Netflix), video conferencing and webinars.

Businesses and other establishments harnessed video conferencing to have meetings online because employees could not travel as before. Webinars became a new norm of online discussions in absence of physical seminars. New apps surfaced (e.g. Zoom) and existing ones (e.g. Google Meetup) customized their products to make webinars easy and cost-effective.

Online platforms and tools, especially of social media, made it possible for governments, health authorities and researchers on one hand and common people on the other to exchange information on a very large scale.

Social networking and content sharing sites (e.g. Facebook, Twitter, YouTube and Instagram) amplified social media usage by serving content based on consumers' browsing behavior. Thus, if you looked for or browsed a message on COVID-19 on Facebook, the platform would serve you a series of messages, resulting in confusion and stress.

A number of surveys have come up in the last one year on how social media has been consumed during the epidemic. Since there are large variations among geographies, and some data is not in the public domain, let me share the one that shows clear trends:

- Social media usage in terms of new subscribers and usage time had slowed down in 2019, but it saw a spike following the pandemic. For example, in surveys till the middle of 2020, about 50% US adults reported increasing social media use. After high growth in the first 4-6 months of the year, it moderated a bit; the growth may temper further in 2021.

- Usage of all social media platforms did not increase uniformly during the pandemic. For example, in the US, the usage of Instagram, Snapchat and Twitter remained static, Facebook increased slightly but TikTok usage increased from an average 2 minutes per day in 2019 to 7 minutes in 2020. Besides TikTok, local apps made a debut and became very popular in a short time in some countries (e.g. Chingari, Mitron, Roposo, and Sharechat in India).

- Creation of video has seen a rise during COVID-19, and respondents in a survey shared that they would continue to create videos post-COVID-19. [ref 70]

- The use of social media for science communication got a big boost during COVID-19. Research journals and health research bodies used social media to directly approach the people. However, in their hurry to reach the masses before others, many researchers published research on public forums and publicized that on social media without peer-review, on small samples, and without explaining context.

- Many brands have learned to leverage social media in times of piled up inventories and a drastic reduction in sales. Smarter among them have used social media to be in touch with existing and potential clients with targeted messages. They are seen using catchy messaging and videos, live and virtual events, association with the social cause of checking the pandemic and other promotional techniques to draw attention and generate sales. Social media is being used also for promoting discounts, sales and flexible terms of payment. Social platforms have come up with features such as e-marketplaces and mobile transactions and help to businesses. As soon as the first wave of pandemic subsided and economic activity started, advertisements on social media platforms also saw a quick rise.

- It is also reported that a good number of younger people who had first lapped up video conferencing/ video chat apps (e.g. Zoom) to be in touch with friends during COVID-19 later shifted to audio apps as they are less intrusive, do not need to keep looking at the screen and yet are more intimate than texting.

Qualitative aspects of social media communication during the pandemic

It does not need emphasis that during the stressful times of COVID-19, television, online media and smartphones gave people a lot in terms of remaining connected, and getting information and entertainment. Even very old people lapped up social media.

Social media not only helped people be in touch with others, it gave people company. About half of the respondents in the US and UK covered in a survey said social media helped them feel less lonely or less anxious/ stressed. [ref 70]

The worry about self-image on social media lessened among teenagers and young adults as they did not go out for socialization as much as before. It is reported that this has continued even after the lifting of lockdown; perhaps a re-think of their priorities during isolation has played a role in this change.

How social media helped in COVID-19 related communication and information dissemination has been discussed above. Let us now see how it led to intentional or unintentional harm.

First, the excess flow of information itself caused mental health issues, especially when the pandemic was in the ascendance and among people who had to stay away from families due to lockdown. People were obsessed with updates, and social media was the best means to get them.

Many surveys have been conducted since the start of the pandemic, and most of them have found a rise in stress due to overuse of social media. For example, a GWI [https://www.globalwebindex.com] study showed that mental health issues had arisen during the pandemic and were continuing, and besides other categories, people spending more than four hours a day on social media were a major group concerned about their mental health. "There are clear correlations between consumption of social media, and online news, with mental health concerns. This is partly to do with their heaviest users being on the young side," the study report says.

Second, the type of content being pushed on social media, even when it was factual, was not helpful. A study conducted during early stage of the pandemic validates this: among the most-watched 100 videos on YouTube on the disease (those associated with the word 'coronavirus') talked about deaths, anxiety, quarantine and travel restrictions, and very few on advisories. [ref 9]

From February 2020 itself, it was clear that information relating to the pandemic was being churned out in more than desirable quantity and not always with good intent, on online and electronic versions of traditional media, websites and social media. Social media entities of even established media houses played one-upmanship in broadcasting information without checking the genuineness of facts and figures. WHO called the phenomenon *infodemic*.

Third, misinformation was rampant on social media, and it hurt people, society and governance systems badly.

Earlier research on the spread of science-related misinformation has shown that those promoting such stories are much more active and they spread their messages much more efficiently than those supporting scientific narratives. They are full of distrust in science and scientific institutions, and this drives them to take extra pains to spread their viewpoints. That applied to COVID-19 in text-book perfection: whenever a pseudo-scientific message was introduced on social media, it spread fast through all possible channels and was shared to the extent that a large WhatsApp group would receive the same message from many members in quick succession. As discussed earlier, people's views on scientific information on the disease were also shaped by their political affiliations.

The spread of misinformation at its rather benign level was used for getting lots of traffic to become popular and/ or make money. The ancient French astrologer Nostradamus was invoked to prove that the pandemic was pre-destined. Astrological predictions were made on the progress and the likely end of the pandemic. Godmen and people engaged in spreading pseudo-sciences had a field day in drawing associations of the disease with whatever looked saleable.

But social media was milked in much more sinister ways by criminals, fraudsters and those wanting to exploit people's worries and helplessness. Disinformation that trended on social media during the pandemic included:

- Creating shortages and spreading rumors about it. Social media was flooded with such messages specially on the eve of lockdowns. Old photos of people standing in long queues for essential items, fights over daily-use provisions and closed stores were posted. Later, when people started hoarding such products (e.g. medicines, face masks, sanitizers, personal protection gear, daily consumables) and real shortages started, messages telling why the supplies will not be forthcoming soon were relayed. That led to panic, which in turn led to people thronging to marketplaces to buy things (thus not bothering about social distancing), queues and actual shortages.

- Sale of personal protection kits illegally in the face of an initial shortage, and sale of sub-standard merchandise (e.g. N-95 face-masks and medicinal herbs) online, with promotion through Facebook ads (the platform responded by screening and restricting ads relating to COVID-19 related products).

- Claims of dubious remedies for killing the virus. Experts were misquoted and fake reports of the success of the treatment were spread as testimonials. A Madagascar brew was sold in black for a hudred times its fair price. Besides fleecing gullible people in a large number, such treatments are reported to have caused direct physical harm to many. For example, a couple was killed in the US after consuming too much hydroxychloroquine. People hurt their throat by taking too hot water and spoiled their digestion by taking too much of spice-broth. Doctors say, since many traditional and home-remedies do not come with contra-indications, they might result in metabolic diseases such as hypertension, diabetic issues and hyperacidity if consumed wrongly.

- Promotion of home-remedies as highly potent. Claims that lemon and hot water killed the virus, and some soups and concoctions boosted immunity enough to ward off the virus spread through social media. Such remedies may have a palliative or curative role but that was exaggerated.

- Utterly wrong associations to create confusion and disharmony. Rumors were spread that some technology or actions being taken by hospitals and governments were leading to the spread of the virus and deaths. In the UK, 5G masts were set on fire after messages with #5GCoronavirus hashtag trended on Twitter. [ref 24]

- Conspiracy theories. Conspiracy theories started with detailed reports with supposed evidence of the Chinese government spreading a lab-created virus. Other stories talked of a group of autocratic world leaders spreading the virus and lockdown to suppress opposition. The development of vaccines and especially the fast approvals given to vaccines were said to be meant for helping pharma companies. Death certificates were said to be manipulated by governments to scare people or to show fewer deaths than actual. Even stories of a 'chip' being inserted in the name of vaccine to track people circulated.

Bill Gates was in the line of attack from people generally critical of him and Microsoft. They made him a culprit in spreading the virus in cahoots with the Chinese, by bringing forth his old video in which he had warned about a possible pandemic. Then they found a deep conspiracy in his supporting vaccination. At one time, he was falsely quoted as having found a spiritual reason behind the pandemic. Without checking the veracity of the quote, some British newspapers and Facebook celebrities spread it far and wide.

Though fact-checks were in place at platform and government levels, the spread of fake news was so fast (sometimes due to a coordinated effort by the interested parties) that it was difficult to stop or counter it. Machine tools were used to check the flow of disinformation based on toxic keywords used. However, faking was often so masterful, with the use of subtle messaging, image manipulation and deep-faking of videos that machines failed to spot it.

There is a lot of reservation among platforms in checking misinformation/ disinformation because any gate-keeping on social media invites the blame of stifling the freedom of expression. Social media monitoring has not only ethical but also commercial implications. This circumspection was visible also during the pandemic. For example, Twitter followed its standard policy on misinformation. It says, it categorizes false information under these three broad categories and takes action accordingly: Misleading information on health is treated strictly and the message is flagged or removed depending on its potential to harm. Disputed claims, where the accuracy, truthfulness or credibility of the claim is contested or unknown, invite flagging or issuing a warning. Unverified claims do not invite action. Some other platforms explained away their actions by referring to their 'freedom of expression' policies and acted only when a strong violation took place.

SOCIAL MEDIA IN DIFFERENT LANGUAGES

SOCIAL MEDIA IN LANGUAGES OTHER THAN ENGLISH

English is the default technical language on the web though it no longer has a monopoly over the content. Initially all the menus on web platforms and websites, URLs and search queries had to be in English but that has given way to other languages in regions where such languages are popular. In fact, French, Spanish and Chinese have been in use on web media for a long time. Implementation of Unicode system has helped the spread of various other languages on the web.

As internet has spread fast in the recent past through smartphones, a very large number of people who cannot write and/ or speak English have joined social media. They like to create content and respond on social media in their mother tongue rather than in English. This has forced social networking and instant messaging platforms to come out with language versions of their apps.

While Facebook, Twitter and WhatsApp are highly popular social media platforms in most parts of the globe – and all of them have enabled socialization in many languages - there are a large number of local and language-centric social media platforms that have mushroomed in countries where English is not the mother-tongue.

For platforms and marketers/ sellers, local languages make sense for many reasons. In some of the largest countries in the world, the local languages are spoken much more than English and the numbers are enormous: There are more than 6 billion people (out of 7.5 billion people on the earth) who do not understand English! Fewer than 1% Chinese speak English and not more than 10% of Indians, Russians and Brazilians can do so. This is a large market as well as a large social base. For politicians, charities, NGOs and celebrities, a huge number of people are waiting to be influenced through messages in their own languages.

Local social networking apps are quite popular among young people who are comfortable and confident in communicating in their lingo more than in English. They are usually less-educated than their English counterparts, more rooted to the ground and not cosmopolitan in outlook and lifestyles. This segment includes youth living in slums, small towns and villages, and unemployed or semi-employed youth. They are also lapped up by housewives, people with lower incomes, and those in low-paid jobs. As compared to people in higher strata of society, this section of people are considered amenable to change in opinion and are also likely to cast their vote. Political parties and leaders in democracies, therefore, make good use of such apps to communicate with voters.

Take India, the second most populated country in the world, where the use of internet and mobile phones is growing fast and the use of social media in local languages is growing even faster. It is estimated that more than half of nearly 450 million social media users in India use a local language as compared to English, and the rate of growth of vernacular social media use is much higher than that of English. So, several social media platforms and apps are being developed every year to meet the communication needs of speakers of non-English languages, some of them [e.g. ShareChat: https://sharechat.com] catering only to native languages. In most of such platforms, you can do all socialization and instantly push your content to global platforms [e.g. WhatsApp, Twitter] too, thus getting the best of both the worlds.

The use of language, like social media itself, in China is unique. The Chinese government has supported local platforms and has been restricting foreign platforms on one or the other pretext. This has resulted in a very strong social media ecosystem in the Chinese language. Some big Chinese platforms are now expanding their base by entering English and other languages.

Breaking the language barrier

All web media, social media in particular, is constantly breaking the language barrier in interesting ways. One is the use of autocorrect, popular acronyms/ abbreviations (e.g. '*OTP*' for *one-time password*), emojis, GIFs (short animations), etc. that make it easy for one to express himself, without being proficient in a language. Two, a mix of languages known to users in a location, local jargon and mis-spellings are not frowned upon on social media. So, one is free to express one's thoughts in broken English mixed with the local language, half sentences, etc. Three, now that pictures and videos are becoming the most used form of content, one need not write much, or at all, and yet express oneself. Hundreds of language-neutral videos trend every day on major social networking and media sharing platforms.

Is English swallowing other languages due to social media?

It has been strongly argued that the fast growth of ICT, especially the web and social media, has made English much more dominant than it was before. English is pervasive on the World Wide Web, codes and URLs are written in English, settings on smartphones and menus on different platforms and apps are usually in English. Even if there are options for use of other languages, there are issues, e.g. changing the default language option and difficulty in writing languages in non-Roman scripts. This dependence upon English reduces people's love for their native languages; when languages are not used for active communication, they tend to decay.

At the same time, since social media users are predominantly non-English speakers, they try to communicate in their local language whenever they can.

Popular non-English languages do not seem to be under any threat anyways, because they are the natural choice for communication due to their popularity. When a language is also used for official communication and as the medium of education at least in lower classes, its use by people is guaranteed. When a local language has a minimum base, it is used also by marketers to sell their products, politicians to get votes, and so on. As discussed above, social apps in native languages are making it easy for non-English languages to communicate smoothly.

Languages that do not have official patronage and do not serve the purpose of earning the bread are at the risk of losing out, and social media might be contributing as an accelerator.

It is interesting to note that social media is quietly leveling the communication barrier that existed between highly educated and less educated or between English-speaking and non-English speaking segments of the population. The new vocabulary is language-neutral and effortlessly enters all languages. Just to give one example, the words *'like'*, *'follow'* and *'download'* have become almost universal and are understood well by all regular users of social media whether they know English or not. Inclusion of such expressions in one's native language perhaps need not be seen as a threat from English.

SOCIAL MEDIA'S INFLUENCE ON LANGUAGES

Social media has made a big influence in the way languages are written and spoken in informal settings. English, being the language that has been used on social media for the longest time, has naturally been impacted the most.

In the initial days of mobile phones, one could send small SMS messages, and typing them with small keyboards was a big problem, so abbreviations of common expressions arose and became universally accepted. Thus, you would type *asap* for 'as soon as possible', *gr8* for 'great' and *lol* for 'laughing out loud', and you would ask *'how u doin bro'* rather than typing out the full sentence, 'How are you doing, brother?'. Some such expressions have got established in day-to-day conversations and even entered dictionaries while others have become less popular or disappeared.

Twitter, with its initial limit of 140 characters per tweet, also contributed to the shortening of words, sentences, even expressions that would usually go beyond one sentence.

Grammar and punctuation have taken a big hit on social media because (i) punctuation marks are on a separate screen on phone keyboards, (ii) the sentences on social media are either small or fragmented, (iii) the comments are spontaneous and instant, and (iv) absence or wrong use of punctuation marks, and wrong grammar, are not frowned upon.

The peculiarities of netiquette and peculiar use of special characters and punctuation marks influence the language in interesting ways. On social media, you would write in ALL CAPS to shout or make a strong statement; use full-stop to *highlight.a.point*; use multiple punctuation marks for showing urgency or a strong emotion – *did you say that???!*; not use capital letters at all, even at the start of a sentence; use special characters such as '@' to refer to a specific person or place; use '#' for a special object/ event; and so on.

Social media is limiting the need for linguistic nuances for expressing emotions and complex thoughts. Emotions are easily taken care of by emojis and GIFs. Long expressions for nuanced thoughts and emotions have hardly a place on social media, long-form blogs being an honorable exception.

The generation gap is evident on social media when it comes to the use of language. Older people usually stay with a more standard language, sometimes with abbreviations that they learned during earlier days, while younger people use jargon and slang. Younger people also like to express themselves with the help of selfies, photographs and videos. The usage and choice of emojis also differ according to age, gender, education, social status, etc.

Ever since internet and then WWW came into being, a new vocabulary has arisen and it is being enriched fast by social media. Old words are also finding new, more popular, meanings. Starting with *internet, smartphone, web, website, chat* and *blog*, we now have *tweet, stream, selfie, livecast, meme, like/ unlike, friend/ unfriend, troll, viral, upvote/ downvote* and hundreds of other new expressions.

Some puritans scoff at the language used on social media and worry about a too casual approach towards the structure and rich vocabulary of established languages. On the other hand, many language experts feel that social media is quickening the *organic evolution* of languages, especially English. In any case, the effect of the language used on social media does not affect mainstream literature, scientific writing or other serious forms of writing.

For general communication, social media is a cauldron where new expressions and ways to express are being cooked every moment. It is difficult to guess whether it eventually leads to a common global language at the expense of linguistic diversity, helps major language to grow together, or something else.

SOCIAL MEDIA AS MASS MEDIA AND MEDIUM OF FREE EXPRESSION

Until Gutenberg established the first printing press in 1440, the only methods of broadcasting information among people were to put notices or banners in public places, send letters through couriers or post, or make announcements through town criers or at public gatherings. The printing press led to mass production of pamphlets, books, newspapers and magazines. The institution of *'press'* thus took shape and later took upon itself the responsibility of questioning the authority on omissions and commissions, and taking up people's cause. In the watchdog role, it came to be regarded as 'the fourth pillar of democracy'. Later came radio and then television. All these media had one thing in common: there was an institution that gathered news, and then took editorial decisions about the content that was to be spread to the masses. Since these could broadcast news to a large number of people, they were collectively termed as *mass media*.

Though diehard traditional communication experts may not fully agree, the World Wide Web changed the concept of mass media, and social media has turned it upside down. In terms of its reach and capacity to broadcast information/ news, social media is far ahead of the traditional mass media. One major difference between the two is that social media lacks the institutional framework of editors that, in the traditional media, comes in between the information and its consumer. Another major difference is that while the traditional media mostly carries out one-way communication, social media communicates in multiple directions.

With the advent of WWW came many websites that gave news, and updated news many times during the day. Then came blogs, which gave a new tool of self-expression to the common man. When blogging was at its peak in advanced countries, people had started depending upon the web for information and news more than newspapers, and some media observers felt that the web media would soon annihilate the mainstream press. The regular press learned to co-exist with the ICT-led media and web media too could not overwhelm the traditional media significantly.

A sort of dynamic equilibrium has now emerged in which traditional media, static websites, portals of mainstream media, blogs, newsfeeds and apps, bookmarking sites, search engines, social networks and instant messaging apps supplement one another while they also fight for space and prominence. For the consumer, this has resulted in 'information overkill'.

When we look at social media from a mass media perspective, we need to note the features that make it more efficient, effective and democratic than the traditional media and some that make it chaotic, irresponsible, superficial and unreliable.

- On social media, the news is created and distributed all the time. It does not wait for a new edition to be printed or a television news bulletin to be broadcast.

- Social media news, unless restricted by authorities or not available because of technical reasons, does not recognize geographic boundaries and is available everywhere.

- Social media is not limited also by the format of the message. The same platform or blog can have text, audio, image, animations and video.

- Most of the information and news is free on the web, including social media.

- In traditional media, the news entity is usually owned by someone with commercial, and possibly other, interests. The editorial line, therefore, is seldom neutral. On social media, there is no central ownership of bloggers, other content creators and commenters, who act as independent publishers.

- The news changes as it changes hands on social media. In most cases, the receiver of news can edit it before sharing it with others.

- On social media, one can make instant comments and give feedback, unlike on newspapers, magazines, radio and television.

- When a large number of news consumers on social networks find a news item worthy of sharing, they themselves become broadcasters. This leads to fast spread of that news item, or it going *viral*. The traditional media can spread news fast to some extent but the virality through instant broadcast by users is not possible.

- Though a blog, a Facebook page or an individual's Twitter feed may be a minuscule entity, social media in totality is enormous. A single news item that has gone viral can cover the news space of a hundred newspapers.

- Social media is also much wider in its range of opinions and shades of news, than all traditional media put together. It is often impetuous, impressionistic, with little knowledge of background, and full of other imperfections.

- Since all traditional media entities also have web editions and they are also active on social media, these versions of theirs have qualities of mainstream media as well as web/ social media. Conversely, many news blogs and news apps are run by editorial and reporting teams, and they compete with web editions of the mainstream press.

- Mainstream and social media borrow from each other. They source news from each other and make use of opinions made on the other. Mainstream media even has sections/ bulletins fully devoted to social media.

- Television and radio channels and media websites routinely pick up photographs and videos of sudden events (e.g. plane crash, road and rail accidents, sudden street fight) posted on social media by eyewitnesses. Social media does not bother about the source of information, and lifts content from everywhere, including mainstream media.

- Many organizations accredit news bloggers as journalists and invite them for press conferences. Bloggers are also invited for product previews and conducted press tours.

- A large number of journalists themselves maintain social media accounts. This helps them in sourcing news, getting new angles for their reports or articles, pre-testing their hypotheses, creating a personal following, and connecting directly with their consumers/ fans.

- Social media is highly reactive. Social media consumers immediately react to what they perceive as a wrong action on the part of powerful people. Besides, there are numerous blogs and other social accounts that relentlessly work for a social or political cause. There are some that create public opinion against governments' wrongdoings. A number of bloggers have been imprisoned or have sacrificed their lives in fighting with governments, criminals and fundamentalists. Thus, social media does play the role of 'the fourth pillar of democracy' though this goes unrecognized. On the other hand, the ethical standards of the mainstream press have generally declined across the globe.

- On social media, the creator or distributor of news can target it to specific audiences much better than the traditional media. Consumers can also customize their news feed by applying filters. They can also choose to share news within closed groups.

- Marketers find web media much more versatile and cost-effective. The per-impression rates for advertisement are usually much lower than those for print and electronic media, and advertisements can be targeted to specific audiences.

- It is much easier to incentivize purchase action on web media than that on traditional media.

- Social media keeps coming out with simple, cost-effective/ free and instant options for the broadcast of news. A number of news apps flash breaking news faster than the apps and websites of traditional media. News aggregators collate news from different sources and serve them with filters and customization to suit individual users. YouTube gives everybody the tool to create one's own video channel and even live telecast events. People often record videos of events suddenly happening before their eyes and flash them on social media much before media reporters reach the spot.

Though social media is routinely used for news-making by the traditional mass media, it is still looked down upon by professional editors. A study of US newspaper editors' ratings of social media as news sources, conducted by Yamamoto *et al* [ref 77] in 2017, showed that traditional journalists and their editors still are not sure of the credibility and usefulness of social media as a credible source of news vis-à-vis institutional sources. It was found that traditional editors are not likely to see *citizen journalism* (=reports submitted to traditional media by people at large) as a good source of news. The older and more experienced a journalist, the more distrust he has on the emerging media as a news source of value. Editors at publicly owned media houses and in more pluralistic communities are more open to social media as compared to others.

It would also be worth exploring how news is consumed on social media today. A Reuters Institute document of 2018 on the use of social media for receiving news, based on data from 40 countries [ref 48], has these salient findings:

- The use of social media for news fell marginally in 2018 in a number of countries, including the US, the UK and France, after years of continuous growth. This was mostly due to a sharp fall in the number of people using Facebook for news, though average Faccbook use has not declined.

- News apps, email newsletters, and mobile notifications continue to gain in importance. However, users in some countries are starting to complain that they are being bombarded with too many messages.

- There is a rise in the use of messaging apps for news. WhatsApp is now used for news in a big way: In Malaysia, 54% of the survey sample used it, in Brazil, 48%.

Matsa and Shearer [ref 44] found in 2018 that about two-thirds of American adults at least occasionally consumed news on social media. However, a majority of them (57%) felt that the news on social media was largely inaccurate. Facebook, followed by YouTube and Twitter were the top platforms on which the highest portion of users was exposed to news.

Globally, the top reasons people use social media across the age groups are to fill up spare time and to stay up-to-date with news and current affairs, says GWI [ref 70]. The other two reasons are to find funny or entertaining content (in the age group up to 37 years) and to stay in touch with what friends are doing (older people). News is consumed on social media by people of all ages, and a survey in the US and the UK suggests that three out of four want the social media platforms to filter out unverified news stories.

Social media and the freedom of expression

Social media, starting with blogging, has given the power to people to express themselves publicly without the need for a physical medium or support of a traditional media entity.

The special qualities of social media as a medium of communication have been discussed in various chapters including at the beginning of this very chapter. In various chapters, we have also discussed the perils attached with such a free medium of expression, the control mechanisms used by governments, individual efforts and activism against the suppression of information, legal limits to the freedom, bloggers being recognized as press persons, and misuse of the freedom by people.

If you are interested in browsing the matter relating to *freedom of expression* in the book, I would refer you especially to these chapters:

- Concerns Relating to Safety & Security, Privacy and Government Control

- Legal Aspects Relating to Social Media, and

- Social Media as Mass Media and Medium of Free Expression (the present chapter).

MISINFORMATION AND FAKE NEWS

There is no doubt that social media is an efficient medium for the spread of information. It gets more efficient in the exchange and spread of false and/or toxic content.

When people talk of such content on social media, they use different terms to describe it according to the type of mischief and intent behind its creation and spread.

All types of information that is false or wrong is called *misinformation*. A subset of misinformation, which is deliberately falsified is *disinformation*. In disinformation, the intent is to mislead and in turn harm persons, brands or organizations. *Fake news* refers to disinformation presented in the garb of news. Though these terms are not the same, they are mostly used as synonyms; in a broad sense, they all refer to false content that is intentionally created and spread with a purpose to harm.

Of course, information is often twisted or parodied for harmless fun, criticism or sarcasm, but that is not fake news, for example in cartoons and stand-up comedies. Similarly, genuine errors in news reporting do not make the news *fake* in the sense of disinformation.

Traditional media organizations themselves twist the news to make it sensational or one-sided for creating controversy and in turn gaining the attention of viewers/ readers, or for serving some commercial/ political purpose. There is also a rising trend in the traditional press to serve advertorials as news, called *'paid news'*. When traditional media falsifies news beyond accepted levels, it commits a sin even bigger than what the term 'fake news' refers to, but the media gets away with it.

It has been documented that even before social media, events such as war, elections and epidemics resulted in huge quantities of fake news. In the social media age, it has become a major concern due to its enormous harm-potential. Governments and regulatory authorities, law and order agencies, social scientists, media watchers, and people in general are worried about it for their own reasons. A 2018 Reuters Institute study [ref 48] revealed that over half (54%) of the respondents it polled agreed or strongly agreed that they were 'concerned about what is real and fake on the web'.

The making and spreading of fake news

Fake news can originate either as a genuine mistake or created deliberately, the latter being much more prevalent than the former. In either case, it is spread out of proportion to exploit it for nefarious purposes.

Motivations behind spreading fake news range from damage to commercial interests of competitors, politics and elections, geopolitics, religious justifications, financial and other crimes to war and terrorism.

For creation of a piece of duplicitous content, genuine content is manipulated by modifying the content to change the substance as well as context. For example, the speaker is misquoted, time-shifting is done, facts are distorted, a half-truth is told. Genuine facts are presented in a way that viewers and readers make biased conclusions.

Images and videos are manipulated with deep-faking tools. Apps are now readily available for manipulating images and videos.

Since facts presented with data look genuine to users, clever data manipulation is done. On graphs, exaggeration or suppression of scale is done; conclusions are drawn from too small or defective samples; parallels are drawn between unrelated data; data is presented in percentages to confuse users; correlations between two events are shown as cause-effect; selected studies are quoted, leaving the unfavorable ones aside; and so on.

Manipulation of facts must serve the intended purpose, so the messages or news is not only *manipulated*, it is made *manipulative*. The manipulations are sometimes done with the sophistication of war 'psy-ops' (=

psychological war operations). The enormous amount of personal data generated on social media platforms, search engines and e-commerce sites is analyzed with sophisticated technological tools and algorithms are created to serve information to users based on this analytics. A huge industry has taken shape in this 'mind-manipulation' especially using social media data and social media platforms.

Social media has made common people a participant in the creation as well as spread of disinformation. Traditionally, spreading news to confuse the enemy army and population has been in use during wars and the cold war. In fact, the word *disinformation* is derived from a term used by the Russian spy agency during the cold war period for the spread of misleading information. So, disinformation spread one way and rather slowly. Now that social media is everywhere, there are millions of people who willingly or unwillingly participate in the creation and propagation of fake news due to impulse or alignment with a particular viewpoint/ ideology or cause.

Since users of social media usually connect with people of similar opinions, they start believing their own stories, and then feel duty-bound to spread them to others too.

People's higher reliance on social media as compared to established sources of news, especially on instant messaging and news apps, is contributing to the spread of all types of news, including fake news. The lack of trust in the traditional media also makes people believe in the counter-narrative being played on social media.

People also become willing partners because fake news is controversial, dramatic or extreme by its very nature; when not, it is made more interesting. Juicy expressions, especially in colloquial tongue, stereotypes, comic exaggerations, spoofs, parallels with mythical characters... such techniques to lure people and induce them to spread it. If the intent is to agitate people, the techniques must result in a crude, provocative product. If the interest is to subtly change public opinion, the product should look innocent so that even adversaries share it just for laugh.

As shared elsewhere, surveys have found that about half of the social media users are concerned about fake news. These show that the other half is not at all concerned. Such people would hardly ever check the authenticity of content that they share and spread, especially when the fake news is well-crafted to look like genuine news. Even the *concerned* half of the population is not discreet all the time. People can be highly indiscreet and adventurous when tempers are high on some topic/ issue.

When the subject is emotive, individual participants tend to make the messages more virulent as they share them.

People's unfounded confidence in their ability to see through fake news may also contribute to its spread, especially when they are opinion leaders. A Pew Research survey found that the majority of American adults felt confident in their ability to spot fake news during the 2016 presidential elections, which is not supported by common observation. A 2018 study by British Broadcasting Corporation in Nigeria, Kenya and India showed that people were generally confident that they could spot fake news while sharing such news without verifying. Instead of checking veracity, people relied on alternative signals such as images and number of comments. When a message was received from friends, they did not check further [ref 10].

In societies that have had major attacks of fake news, people may become suspicious when a piece of information looks unreal. So, the fake news creators have to invest a lot of energy in crafting and spreading it. In places where internet and social media entered recently through smartphones, people tend to believe and share information as it comes to them; in such societies, even crude fake news circulates unchallenged and unhindered on social media.

People and organizations aligned with a particular belief/ ideology are found to be engaged perpetually in fake news so as to influence others into their way of thinking. Extreme right-wing thinkers, white supremacists, fundamentalists, racists and fans of warring teams are some such though-related groups and organizations. In a study on the spread of fake information on childhood vaccination on Facebook [ref 14], it was found that anti-vaccination groups have been active to spread false information on vaccination, acting as echo-chambers and thus reinforcing the content created by just a few authors. The study also found that advertisements with links on social media help dissemination of such information, and conversely, an action on the part of the platform to stop such advertisements leads to a dramatic decline in its spread.

Micro-targeting is now being used widely for influencing vulnerable target groups. Since these groups are distributed, usually non-political and sometimes closed to the general public, promoting political views this way does not come on the radar of fact-checking teams or monitoring tools employed by the platforms or regulatory authorities.

Citizens of nations at war keep constantly fighting each other on social media, with disinformation in a variety of forms, provocative statements, memes and emojis, distorted history, warnings and threats.

People whose interests are served by attacking minorities based on their special identities (e.g. gender, religion, race, skin color, country of origin in case of immigrants, language) are known to be a major category of fake news purveyors. Since they get natural support from the majority in the society, such fake news is easy to spread.

In India, a pattern has developed in which fake news is started and spread by an interested group through social media. When people are incensed and tempers are raised on social media, the other group retaliates and exchanges become more and more ugly. Then people come out in the streets, sloganeering happens, stones are pelted, and it all culminates in the burning of public property, injuries and even deaths.

Rumors of child lifting that spread through WhatsApp caused lynching of 40 people by mobs across India in 2018. There was a visible trend to these killings: a message was spread on WhatsApp that some strangers were roaming in the area to abduct children. Then, some stranger – a tourist or one from a different locality – would be spotted, a crowd would gather and people would start hitting the victim. It did not stop until the stranger was brutally maimed or killed – by people who would generally be peace-loving and not approve of harming an innocent.

Institutional fake news creators usually do not depend too much on laypeople and supporters, at least not until the fake news has reached a critical mass necessary for viral propagation. They use human armies as well as automation tools and bots, hijack or phish social media entities, pay celebrities to align with disinformation.

Many times, servers in foreign countries and hidden with the help of technology are used for the creation and spread of disinformation.

Andrus Ansip, former vice-president of the European Commission is reported to have stated that Russia spends at least $1.2 billion a year on pro-Kremlin media to create disinformation. In addition, significant spending on pumping out misinformation has been detected during elections in at least 18 countries. During the pre-Brexit referendum, many entities are reported to have spent significant sums in spreading misinformation to influence public opinion.

It has also been reported that it is becoming progressively easy and inexpensive to buy fake followers and organize disinformation campaigns.

One can see hundreds of people selling misinformation packages for sums as little as $10 on freelancing sites such as Fiverr.

Impact of fake news on individuals, society and systems

Disinformation or fake news can do serious harm not only to individuals but also to the social fabric, politics and national security.

People's reputations have been damaged, careers have been finished. Frauds have been committed and election debates have been derailed. Riots have been instigated overnight. People have been killed in many countries by spreading racial and communal hatred and other forms of fake news.

Vigilantism or taking the law into one's hands and delivering justice according to one's notions is too bad for the society. It becomes uglier and more wicked when it goes online. Certain individuals or groups with extreme notions of right and wrong start trolling and shaming people who are supposed to have committed crimes or sins. They resort to spreading rumors about their targets, and in many cases, the targets then become victims of real-life abuse and violence.

Fake news often attacks the vulnerable points in society and plays with people's emotions, sometimes with hatred towards the dominant class. For example, in developing countries with wide-spread economic disparity or in traditional societies with a number of identities or in nations where governments are seen to be corrupt and power concentrated in a few hands, it is very easy to create a fake news item (in text, images, even video) that pits the fake news victim against the poor, a particular caste/ race/ ethnic group, or the common man. Even when the one receiving such content feels that it might not be true, he feels so strongly aligned with the poor or one race or the suffering common man that he becomes a willing partner in making the disinformation more virulent and spreading it.

In India, in 2017-18, people calling themselves protectors of the cow (the cow is considered sacred in Hindu religion) spread a rumor on Facebook and WhatsApp against people engaged in the transportation of cows and in the business of beef and cowhide, which resulted in wide-spread violence against them.

In Nigeria, many people were reported to be killed and properties gutted in 2018 when violent images with wrong association with a religious group and call for retaliation were spread on Facebook.

A UN fact-finding mission looking into large-scale killings of Rohingya Muslims in Myanmar in 2016-17 found that Facebook was exploited by ultra-right Buddhists in spreading hate, which resulted in massacres and over 650,000 Rohingyas taking refuge in neighboring Bangladesh. Yanghee Lee, the Special Rapporteur of the UN on human rights in Myanmar is quoted as having said that Facebook 'had turned into a beast'.

People also become victims of fake information when they are in distress. For example, a person suffering from a chronic ailment whose treatment is not responding, is painful or is very costly would keep on searching for alternate medicine. He is likely to be deeply influenced when he finds a doctor's video full of half-truths, pseudo-scientific logic and fake testimonials on how his medicine works wonders. In desperation, he would follow the doctor's advice, which would include buying medicine or equipment from him. This becomes even more believable when one's friends share such content on chat apps with the intent to either help the needy or get a commission out of the sale.

A Baltimore University and CHEQ study [ref 8] estimated in 2019 the global cost of fake news as $78 billion a year on account of stock market losses, financial misinformation, reputation loss, causing public health issues, harm to online safety, etc. The estimate is conservative and adds up only the main areas in which losses occur in major countries. Indirect losses (e.g. of loss of trust and transparency) are not even countable in financial terms.

Starting end-2020, retail investors traded in large numbers in Wall Street, the US stock market, on the recommendations and inspirations shared on social media, particularly on Reddit. Market prices of many penny stocks rose to unsustainable levels due to herd-buying. Though such market manipulations have occurred earlier, even on much larger scales, this time social media had a big role in spreading the frenzy.

During COVID-19 and recent national elections in major democracies, fake news had a field day.

Since social media is now the main channel for fake news, this activity negates a lot of what social media contributes to individuals, society and systems.

Action against fake news on social media

Before the enormous rise of social media, fake news usually emanated from sources that could be identified and tracked. In the initial days of social media too, when it consisted just of blogs, forums and limited social networking – and when smartphones and internet penetration was yet low – checking fake news was easy and its harm-potential was also limited. Omnipresent social networking and content sharing has changed it all.

Much of the social media today is platform-based. So, theoretically, it should be possible for the platforms to easily identify and stop fake news. We discussed earlier the enormity of fake news messages and the faking becoming sophisticated; yet, modern technologies should make it possible to identify and control disinformation. Besides, major social media platforms are rich enough to employ thousands of people for a fact-check. Surveys across countries have found that most people believe that platforms have the biggest responsibility to fix the problem of fake news. But are they doing enough?

Many reports are available on the web telling how social media networks (especially Facebook) have been casual about sharing consumer data with others. Many cases of huge data leaks from their servers have also occurred. Only now, under pressure from government regulators, parliaments and courts have started taking some actions to ensure the privacy of data and to take responsibility for the content.

Major social media platforms – specifically Facebook, Instagram, YouTube, Twitter and WhatsApp - swear by their policies on filtering and removing inappropriate content, and they sometimes run online and offline campaigns for educating users. For example, Facebook has shared that it removes millions of messages with inappropriate content every quarter. In the second quarter of 2020 (before the 2020 US presidential election), it claims to have removed 22.5 million pieces of hate speech. It also has banned thousands of accounts spreading white supremacy theories and anti-Semitic content. Twitter has said that in the aftermath of rioters taking over the Capitol in the US in January 2021, it found a number of users with multiple accounts to spread misinformation. It removed over 70,000 accounts spreading 'harmful QAnon-associated content' and conspiracy theories. Conversations carrying the following types of activities/ content were specially screened out: coordinated harmful activity, hurt to civic integrity, hateful conduct, glorification of violence, violent threats and sensitive media. Other platforms have also come out with data that shows that they indeed keep flagging or removing harmful content.

Yet, experts feel that they are not serious enough in cleaning the platforms mostly due to commercial reasons.

It is also a fact that tech companies have hidden under various provisions to claim immunity from a legal action arising out of inappropriate content on their platforms. Various national regulatory authorities and parliamentary bodies have questioned them, and lawsuits have been filed but they have generally escaped unhurt seriously. There are unconfirmed reports that in the face of intransigence on the part of these companies, the US government is proposing to revoke Section 230 of the Communications Decency Act, a part of US law that grants liability protections to tech companies for the content on their platforms.

Social media platforms are also criticized for unfairness in filtering out toxic content especially when it comes to people in high positions. In a spat between Twitter and the Indian government, the latter accused of applying different standards in the US and India when it comes to blocking similar content; it was said that while Twitter was critical of protesters storming into US parliament, it allowed dangerous disinformation from those supporting protests in India at that time. Twitter, however, defended its action citing its commitment to the freedom of expression.

Without taking a position in the above instance, let us note that social media has indeed become the most important medium to give expression to people's views and thus serves a *public* function. The platforms' role in filtering content thus comes in direct conflict with privacy as well as the freedom of expression. Moreover, facts and opinions are too nuanced and value-driven to be categorized as good or bad by a bunch of people or machines.

Critics say that social media platforms should not be allowed to run away from their responsibility. They must evolve mechanisms to ensure that at least the universally-accepted inappropriate content is filtered out, and political or commercial considerations do not come in their way in doing that. They can and actually do so, as we have witnessed to a good extent during recent elections and the COVID-19 pandemic.

Then comes the role of governments and law-enforcement agencies in checking fake news. If we consider that, leaving aside the political angle for a moment, disinformation is harmful, we cannot deny authorities a role in checking it. Perhaps, in an ideal situation, these authorities should be non-partisan and represent wisdom in the fields of public policy and governance, working of the human society and technology. In practice, the role is taken up by government bodies or agencies appointed by/ affiliated with the government.

Governments' check on social media, without doubt, is a two-way sword. In an imperfect world, the sword would harm oneself too, however much we try to avoid that. I have discussed the chances of government control and misuse of social media in <u>Concerns Relating to Safety & Security, Privacy and Government Control</u> and <u>Social Media Beyond Personal Socialization</u> chapters, so let us limit the present discussion to how governments are faring when it comes to checking fake news.

All governments seem to be taking action against fake news, but they are rarely successful except where creators of such information are identified. Even if action is taken against people and organizations, they surface again in new avatars. Automation through codes and bots makes it easy for them to multiply their actions afresh.

In democracies, things become difficult for elected governments. Since thousands of lay social media users become an unwitting party in the spread of fake information, action against such a large number of broadcasters can be politically counter-productive and therefore authorities avoid taking mass action. Governments are also wary of touching fake news except where it hurts them. For example, in times of war or terror attack, fake news spreads fast in the garb of nationalism, which usually suits the government in power.

In times of a major event (e.g. war, election, terror attack, epidemic, major natural disaster), authorities as well as platforms are unable to check the proliferation of fake news because millions of messages are shared every minute, especially in countries with a large population active on social media. So, governments and police forces in many countries are seen routinely blocking social networking sites and internet, and picking up some prominent faces for action.

China has used the prevalence of fake news on global social networking platforms as one pretext to block them. In Russia, a law has been enacted in 2019, which makes the spreading of fake news illegal. Free-press activists suspect the intention behind the law, as it gives excessive power in the hands of prosecutors.

In its global misinformation resource page, Poynter [ref 35] has documented that a large number of national and provincial governments have enacted laws or created task forces to check fake news. The paper highlights the conflict of misinformation control with the freedom of expression, and the resultant confusion about the line to be adopted. Freedomhouse [https://freedomhouse.org] regularly comes out with reports showing how governments themselves create a lot of disinformation and on the other hand suppress freedom of information in the name of fake news.

On the other hand, when people have trust in the government and fake news is generally seen to be harming society, people feel that the government should intervene to stop fake news. In a Reuters Institute study mentioned earlier [ref 48], this trend was prominent, especially in Europe (60% of respondents said so) and Asia (63%).

Dealing with fake news, even when there is consensus about the content, is becoming difficult to filter due to many factors such as the nuanced nature of messaging, powerful agencies behind it, a large number of people adopting it, and the use of technology for masquerading it as genuine and harmless content.

It is also seen that agencies or groups behind a fake news attack apply shoot and scoot techniques: they spread the fake news far and wide and in different variations and quietly withdraw. The fake news spreads on its own, and authorities and platforms are unable to track the source.

Misinformation in specific situations has been discussed in other chapters too: For a discussion on the extent of fake news and how it was being checked in elections, please visit Use of social media in democratic politics and elections section in Social Media Beyond Personal Socialization chapter. How fake news on social media presented a challenge during the COVID-19 pandemic in 2020-21 is presented in COVID-19 and social media section of Impact of Social Media on Individual Lives and the Society chapter.

GLOSSARY

<u>Affiliate</u> (In web marketing terms): A blog or website that gets paid a commission for selling others' products through its own efforts, e.g. by putting an advertisement.

<u>Algorithm</u>: A set of rules. Search engines use complex algorithms to serve relevant search results in response to queries.

<u>Analytics</u>: Finding meaningful patterns in data; data interpretation.

<u>Anchor text</u>: Text that is hyperlinked to another entity.

<u>App</u>: A small computer application; on mobile phones, a stand-alone program.

<u>Augmented reality</u> (AR): Putting virtual (unreal but created digitally) objects in real life. The user's reality is augmented as he feels or sees something that is not actually there. Through AR, you could create a coffee mug next to yours or project a piece of art on your wall. (Related: <u>Virtual reality</u>)

<u>Blockchain</u>: A technology in which transactional information is stored in unique segments, called 'blocks', which are instantly available on the internet and can be made part of any 'chain' with the help of cryptography, to make a permanent record of the transaction. Several features such as timestamping, anonymity, multiple copies of the same block, and no single server to store a block make the technology highly secure.

<u>Blog</u> (Construction followed by compression from *web* + *log*): A website published on the World Wide Web, whose main content is in the form of posts that are updated over time and are usually arranged reverse chronologically. *To blog* is to maintain a blog, to post on a blog or to engage in interaction on blogs or other social media accounts.

<u>Blogger</u>: A person who maintains a blog. Also refers to a popular blogging platform [https://blogger.com].

<u>Blogging</u>: The act/ process/ activity of maintaining a blog.

<u>Blogosphere</u>: All blogs, or the blogging community, world-wide or limited by location, interest or other such criteria. Examples: The blogosphere is full of nasty blogs. The Chinese blogosphere is very active these days.

<u>Citizen journalist</u>: A person who is not a journalist by profession but sends reports on events to mainstream media or publishes them on the web.

<u>Comment spam</u>: Bogus, unwanted comments, mostly served through automated software tools. (Related: <u>Spam</u>)

<u>Comment</u>: A response to an article or message, e.g. a comment on a blog post or Facebook post.

<u>Content Management System (CMS)</u>: Software that helps manage digital content, e.g. website, by presenting a user interface for common functions. Examples: Wordpress, Joomla.

<u>Content marketing</u>: Marketing support through publishing content that creates goodwill for a product or service and indirectly encourages people to buy it.

<u>Copyright</u>: The right of the creator on his creation that could be in text, audio, image or audio-visual formats or a computer code.

<u>Creative Commons</u>: A not-for-profit organization giving licenses of different types to creators of content so that users know the exact terms and conditions for using that content.

<u>CSS</u> (=Cascading Style Sheets): A language used for sprucing up HTML documents. Since formatting of content using HTML tags is not efficient, CSS is widely used for this purpose either within the same web page or through a linked external CSS file.

<u>Cybersecurity</u>: Security of the cyberspace.

<u>Cyberspace</u>: All the virtual space created by connected computing devices.

<u>Domain name</u>: Name of the domain.

Domain: Place or location. In web terms, a domain is the place of a website on the World Wide Web.

Downvote: To give a negative vote to a post or comment on social media. Opposite of Upvote.

Dox: To broadcast someone's private information with malicious intent.

Duplicate content: Content found in more than one place on the web. Since it gives the signal that at least one of the available versions is not original, duplicate content is not liked by search engines.

Edublog: A blog for educational purposes.

Emoji (e + moji for picture in Japanese): Pictographs or small pictures for expressing feelings, etc. on social media.

Emoticon: Use of letter, digits and punctuation marks to express feelings. They were popular before picture versions (emojis) came into being on social media. :) is the emoticon for a smiling face while :(for a frowny face. (Related: Emoji)

Enterprise social networking (ESN): Use of social networking within a business enterprise. It usually is part of a social network customized for that business and allows employees to communicate within that firm.

Fair use: Use of copyrighted material allowed for some purposes such as review, news reporting, etc.

Feed (In web terms): An automated system of providing data updates. Feeds are used for data aggregation, news syndication, etc. (Related: Atom, RSS, Newsfeed)

GIF: A type of digital picture, which is amenable to animation. In social media context: very small video clips or animations, which are used for expressing feelings, etc. on social media. GIFs used for this purpose usually show dramatic expressions and may use cartoon characters.

Hashtag: The # symbol. On social media, # is used for tagging a web entity (e.g. a post, image, comment) with a specific term (e.g. an event, a cause, a person) to show association with it.

Hosting (of websites): Please see Web hosting.

HTML (=Hyper Text Markup Language): The language of the web. All web pages are written in HTML because web browsers can interpret content written on an HTML page and serve it to humans. Other web languages can be used for adding features and functionalities to HTML pages.

HTTP (=Hyper Text Transfer Protocol): The set of rules that govern communication of data over the World Wide Web through internet.

HTTPS (=HTTP Secure): HTTP with security. This helps in secure communication over computer networks/ internet.

Hyperlink: Usually called 'link', it refers to the association between an element on a web page and another element anywhere else on the web, including on the same page. When a person clicks on an expression or a visual that is 'hyperlinked' or 'linked' to another web page or element, it opens that web page/ element on the browser.

IGTV (=Instagram TV): Vertical format video on Instagram so that it can be seen on mobile phones without tilting the device.

Infodemic(=information+epidemic): Fast and excessive spread of misinformation.

Internet Service Provider (=ISP): An organization that provides internet services.

Internet: The global network of computers with underlying infrastructure and technologies. (also abbreviated as 'the net') (Related: World Wide Web)

IP address: (IP= Internet Protocol) Address of any entity on the internet. (Related: Domain name, URL)

Javascript: A scripting language, which is often used to add interactivity and other functions on web pages. (It can perform other functions too.)

<u>Keyword</u> (In terms of SEO): The word or phrase that is used by people for web search. In a long search query, keyword refers to the 'key' part that represents the subject of the search.

<u>Link exchange</u> (or *link farm*): A network of websites that hyperlink to one another, mostly to show to search engines a higher link value of such websites.

<u>Link</u>: Please see <u>Hyperlink</u>.

<u>Long-tail keyword</u>: Keyword that is more than one word long and explains the search intent or specifies the exact search subject rather than being generic.

<u>Meme</u>: An image, a short video clip, a quote or some other titbit that spreads fast over social media because it is [usually] funny, interesting or sarcastic and highlights a peculiarity of something or somebody.

<u>Micro-blogging</u>: Regular posting of content in a very short form on social media. Twitter is a popular micro-blogging site.

<u>Micro-targeting</u>: The targeting of messages to small groups on social media.

<u>Mom blog/ Mommy blog</u>: A blog maintained usually by mothers on matters relating to pregnancy, rearing children, child health and parenting.

<u>Monetization</u>: Converting an entity into currency. In online moneymaking parlance, it refers to converting content into earnings.

<u>New media</u>: All forms of digital media, as against traditional media such as newspapers and magazines, books, radio and television. These include all forms of online media and also other digital media.

<u>Newsfeed</u>: The stream of the latest posts presented on social accounts. The posts shown on the newsfeed are from the accounts one follows and those served by the platform. On most social networking accounts, this is served on the homepage and is the first thing that the user sees when he logs in to the website/ app. (Related: <u>Feed</u>)

<u>Omnichannel</u>: In marketing terms, it is the approach that uses all available online and offline channels, as against concentrating on only one marketing channel.

<u>Optimization</u>: The act of making something perform to its optimum level. Websites can be optimized for search, design, fast loading etc. (Related: <u>Search Engine Optimization</u>)

<u>Organic search results</u>: Search results that a search engine delivers due to their relevance to the search query; not paid search results.

<u>PBN</u> (=Private Blog Network): A network of blogs, often expired ones with good link value, which are used for back-linking with particular blogs/ websites to pass on link value. PBNs are not considered a natural way of search engine optimization.

<u>Permalink</u> (=Permanent link): The URL of a post or other web entity, which does not change over time.

<u>PHP</u> (recursive acronym: *'PHP: Hypertext Preprocessor'*; originally PHP= 'Personal Home Page'): A scripting language used in association with HTML to serve web pages with a high level of functionality. Can also be used for programming beyond websites.

<u>Pin</u>: To stick a post or message at a specified position (usually on top) on a website, so that it does not move when the page is scrolled up or down. In Pinterest, 'pin' is a picture that is placed on one's pinboard.

<u>Plugin</u> (In programming terms): A piece of software that is added to the main program to add functionalities.

<u>Public domain</u>: The space available to all. In copyright terms, a creation in 'public domain' is one for which there is no copyright and therefore can be used by anybody without a license or permission.

<u>RSS</u> (=Really Simple Syndication): A form of feed that automatically pulls part or full content from different web pages. RSS thus removes the need to go to individual websites and pull their content. *RSS reader* applications are then used for presenting the content in human-readable form. Atom is another popular feed format. (Related: <u>Feed</u>, <u>Atom</u>)

<u>Search engine optimization</u> (=SEO): Techniques used for showing the value of websites and web pages to search engines. In other words, SEO includes actions involved in improving the visibility and relevance of websites and web pages to search engines.

<u>Server</u> (In web hosting terms): A computer or program dedicated to serving (= supplying) resources. A web host has application servers, firewall servers, data servers, mail servers, etc.

<u>Slacktivism (slack +activism): Supporting a social or political cause with little physical effort, e.g. on social media or through online petitioning (as against physically participating in street protests, etc).</u>

<u>Smiley</u> (pron: smy-lee): Picturization of a smiling face, often used to express happiness and agreement. The typical smiley looks like this: ☺

<u>Snap</u> (in Snapchat): a small video clip.

<u>Social bookmarking</u>: Labeling of socially shared content as important. It is mostly done through social bookmarking sites such as Digg, Reddit and StumbleUpon.

<u>Social commerce</u>: Trading by individuals on social media, goods and services of firms or those provided by aggregating platforms.

<u>Social listening</u>: Monitoring and analyzing conversations on social media so as to get actionable feedback. [Used for business purposes.]

<u>Social media</u>: The online system of creation and sharing of information, with a social (as against individual) element. Social actions include re-sharing of content, commenting, tagging, upvoting and downvoting. Social media includes social sharing of content, blogs, forums, social bookmarking platforms and social networks. (Related: <u>Social network</u>)

<u>Social media influencer</u>: A person who has an exceptionally large number of friends and/ or followers on social media.

<u>Social media marketing</u>: Use of social media in marketing of products and services. Includes promotion and other communication with customers.

Social network: An online community in which creation and sharing of content take place, replete with social actions such as re-sharing of content, commenting, tagging, upvoting and downvoting.

Social networking platforms: Websites that are used for social networking, e.g. Facebook, Twitter, Instagram, Google Plus. (Related: Social media)

Social sharing: Sharing of content on social media entities. On blogs/ websites, it is mostly achieved automatically or manually by the creator of the content; visitors share content mostly through buttons or links provided alongside the content by the user or the social networking platform.

Spam (Also used as verb.): Unwanted junk messages sent through email, comments and other ways. Spam is often sent *en masse* through automated systems. Spamming is done to broadcast a message far and wide or get backlinks.

Tag (in HTML): The opening and closing markup of an HTML element. The opening tag starts with '<' and the closing one ends with '>'. HTML element can loosely be called *code*.

Timeline: A social media account's personal feed. It usually contains the user's own posts and actions taken by him on the account.

Troll (Also used as verb.): A person who posts inflammatory messages on social media (including forums, chat groups and blogs) with a view to provoke others and derail the discussion.

Upvote: To give a positive vote (to a post or comment) on social media. Opposite of Downvote.

URL (=Universal Resource Locator): The address of an entity on the World Wide Web (same as *web address*).

Viral (In social media terms): Highly popular in a short time. When something goes/ becomes *viral*, it has been shared a large number of times in a short period.

Virtual reality (VR): Creating a simulated environment through the use of computer technology. The user feels as if he is part of a virtual, unreal, environment. It is usually achieved through VR gears. (Related: Augmented reality)

Web 2.0: The second generation in the evolution of World Wide Web. Formats that are interactive and sharable are included in web 2.0 as against passive websites of the first generation.

Web hosting: Hosting of websites on the web. The *web host* or the company that hosts websites has a set of servers in which the websites are placed. These host servers must always remain connected to internet.

Webinar (web + seminar): Online panel discussion. The term is also loosely used for webcast of other stage events.

Web media: Online media as against traditional media. This is a general term meant to include all means of information dissemination through the web. (Related: New media)

Weblog: Please see Blog.

Web page: A stand-alone page on the web with its own URL. A website is made up of one or many web pages. (Related: Page)

White-hat SEO: Search engine optimization techniques that are ethical and follow policies considered appropriate by search engines. (Opposite: Black-hat SEO)

Wiki: A collaborative website, often part of a collection, with usually a standard format of an index, segments, information with citations and supporting images, and a simple design. Any user, with minor permissions, can edit a *wiki*. Wiki engine, a form of CMS, is used for writing wikis. Wikipedia [https://en.wikipedia.org] pages are the best example of wikis.

World Wide Web (=www; the web): The system that holds all resources on the internet.

REFERENCES

1. Altitude (2016). The Omnichannel Evolution Of Customer Experience: https://www.altitude.com/resources/omnichannel-evolution-of-customer-experience

2. Amnesty International (2018). Online Violence Against Women: https://www.amnesty.org/en/latest/research/2018/03/online-violence-against-women-chapter-1

3. Anderson, Monica (2018). A Majority of Teens have Experienced some form of Cyberbullying. Pew Research Center: https://www.pewinternet.org/2018/09/27/a-majority-of-teens-have-experienced-some-form-of-cyberbullying

4. Anderson, Monica and Jiang, Jingjing (2018). Teens' Social Media Habits and Experiences. Pew Research Center: https://www.pewinternet.org/2018/11/28/teens-social-media-habits-and-experiences

5. Anderson, Monica *et al* (2018). Activism in the Social Media Age, Pew Research Center: https://www.pewinternet.org/2018/07/11/activism-in-the-social-media-age

6. Australian Psychological Society (2017). Teens need more guidance using social media to avoid harm, psychologists say: https://psychology.org.au/About-Us/news-and-media/Media-releases/2017/Teens-need-more-guidance-using-social-media-to-avo

7. Auxier, Brooke (2020). Activism on social media varies by race and ethnicity, age, political party. Pew Research Center: https://www.pewresearch.org/fact-tank/2020/07/13/activism-on-social-media-varies-by-race-and-ethnicity-age-political-party

8. Baltimore University and CHEQ (2019). The Economic Cost of Bad Actors on the Internet: https://s3.amazonaws.com/media.mediapost.com/uploads/EconomicCostOfFakeNews.pdf

9. Basch *et al* (2020). Preventive Behaviors Conveyed on YouTube to Mitigate Transmission of COVID-19: Cross-Sectional Study. NCBI: https://www.ncbi.nlm.nih.gov/pmc/articles/PMC7124952

10. BBC (2018). Nationalism a Driving Force Behind Fake News in India, Research Shows: https://www.bbc.com/news/world-46146877

11. Beauchamp *et al* (2019). Social Media is Rotting Democracy From Within. Vox: https://www.vox.com/policy-and-politics/2019/1/22/18177076/social-media-facebook-far-right-authoritarian populism

12. Bickert, Monika (2020). Removing Holocaust Denial Content. Facebook: https://about.fb.com/news/2020/10/removing-holocaust-denial-content

13. Bloomberg (2018). A Global Guide to State-sponsored Trolling: https://www.bloomberg.com/features/2018-government-sponsored-cyber-militia-cookbook

14. Bradshaw, Samantha *et al* (2018). Challenging Truth and Trust: A Global Inventory of Organized Social Media Manipulation. University of Oxford: https://blogs.oii.ox.ac.uk/comprop/research/cybertroops2018

15. Bradshaw, Samantha; Bailey, Hannah; and Howard, Philip N. (2021). Industrialized Disinformation: 2020 Global Inventory of Organized Social Media Manipulation: https://comprop.oii.ox.ac.uk/wp-content/uploads/sites/127/2021/01/CyberTroop-Report20-FINALv.3.pdf

16. Bromium (2019) [secondary access]. Social Media Platforms and the Cybercrime Economy: https://www.bromium.com/social-media-platforms-cybercrime-economy

17. Burrows, Thomas (2019). Pervs' Playground: Kids as young as eight being groomed by predators on TikTok app that is more popular than Snapchat. The Sun: https://www.thesun.co.uk/news/8453441/kids-as-young-as-8-being-groomed-by-sick-predators-on-tiktok-app-that-is-more-popular-than-snapchat

18. CareerBuilder (2018). More Than Half of Employers Have Found Content on Social Media That Caused Them NOT to Hire a Candidate: http://press.careerbuilder.com/2018-08-09-

More-Than-Half-of-Employers-Have-Found-Content-on-Social-Media-That-Caused-Them-NOT-to-Hire-a-Candidate-According-to-Recent-CareerBuilder-Survey

19. Chiou, Lesley and Tucker, Catherine (2018). Fake News and Advertising on Social Media: A Study of the Anti-Vaccination Movement. NBER Working Paper no. 25223: https://www.nber.org/papers/w25223

20. Clegg, Nick (2021). Referring Former President Trump's Suspension From Facebook to the Oversight Board. Facebook: https://about.fb.com/news/2021/01/referring-trump-suspension-to-oversight-board

21. Cobrapost (2019). Operation Karaoke: https://cobrapost.com/blog/Operation-Karaoke/1413

22. Confessore *et al* (2018). The Follower Factory. The New York Times: https://www.nytimes.com/interactive/2018/01/27/technology/social-media-bots.html

23. Congress Foundation (2018). Congress-30: https://www.congressfoundation.org/projects/congress-30

24. Content Marketing Institute (2020). B2B Content Marketing 2020: https://contentmarketinginstitute.com/wp-content/uploads/2019/10/2020_B2B_Research_Final.pdf

25. Cybermum India (2018). Be the Child On Children's Day – Try Out Role Reversal To Build Better Bonds With Your Kids: https://cybermumindia.wordpress.com/2018/11/15/be-the-child-on-childrens-day-try-out-role-reversal-to-build-better-bonds-with-your-kids

26. Cybermum India (2018). McAfee Survey: Parents Share Pictures of Their Kids Online, Despite Understanding the Risks Involved: https://securingtomorrow.mcafee.com/consumer/mcafee-survey-parents-share-pictures-of-their-kids-online-despite-understanding-the-risks-involved

27. Das, Ronnie and Ahmed, Wasim (2020). Despite concerns, COVID-19 shows how social media has become an essential tool in the democratisation of knowledge. LSE: https://blogs.lse.ac.uk/impactofsocialsciences/2020/06/05/despite-concerns-covid-19-shows-how-social-media-has-become-an-essential-tool-in-the-democratisation-of-knowledge

28. Dibb, Bridget (2019). Social media Use and Perceptions of Physical Health. Heliyon, vol. 5, issue 1: https://www.heliyon.com/article/e00989

29. D'Urso, Joey (2020). How the coronavirus pandemic is changing social media. Reuters Institute: https://reutersinstitute.politics.ox.ac.uk/risj-review/how-coronavirus-pandemic-changing-social-media

30. EC (2019). Social media - statistics on the use by enterprises: https://ec.europa.eu/eurostat/statistics-explained/index.php/Social_media_-_statistics_on_the_use_by_enterprises

31. Edison Research (2019). The Infinite Dial 2019: https://www.edisonresearch.com/infinite-dial-2019

32. Facebook (February, 2021). Ad Library: https://www.facebook.com/ads/library

33. Folha de S.Paulo (2018). Empresários bancam campanha contra o PT pelo WhatsApp: https://www1.folha.uol.com.br/poder/2018/10/empresarios-bancam-campanha-contra-o-pt-pelo-whatsapp.shtml

34. Freedomhouse (2019). Freedom in the World 2019: https://freedomhouse.org/report/freedom-world/freedom-world-2019

35. Funke, Daniel and Flamini, Daniela (2018) [updated; accessed 2021]. A guide to anti-misinformation actions around the world. Poynter: https://www.poynter.org/ifcn/anti-misinformation-actions

36. GovLoop (2018). How Governments are using Social Media Today: https://www.govloop.com/how-governments-are-using-social-media-today

37. Grinberg, Nir *et al* (2019). Fake news on Twitter during the 2016 US presidential election. Science, vol 363: https://science.sciencemag.org/content/363/6425/374

38. IAMAI. Social Media and Lok Sabha Elections: https://cms.iamai.in/Content/ResearchPapers/670023f4-e2e3-4ec5-9d97-18a4ec5aeeb5.pdf

39. Jin, Kang-Xing (2020). Keeping People Safe and Informed About the Coronavirus. Facebook: https://about.fb.com/news/2020/12/coronavirus

40. Kaltheuner and Weatherhead (2018). How Facebook Tracks You on Android: https://media.ccc.de/v/35c3-9941-how_facebook_tracks_you_on_android

41. Kelly *et al* (2018). Social Media Use and Adolescent Mental Health: Findings From the UK Millennium Cohort Study. EClinicalMedicine, vol 6: https://www.sciencedirect.com/science/article/pii/S2589537018300609

42. Levinson-Waldman, Rachel (2018). Government Monitoring of Social Media: Legal and Policy Challenges. The Brennan Center for Justice: https://www.brennancenter.org/analysis/government-monitoring-social-media-legal-and-policy-challenges

43. Marengo *et al* (2018). Highly-visual Social Media and Internalizing Symptoms in Adolescence. Computers in Human Behavior, vol 82: https://www.sciencedirect.com/science/article/pii/S0747563218300037

44. Matsa, Katerina Eva and Shearer, Elisa (2018). News Use Across Social Media Platforms 2018. Pew Research Center: https://www.journalism.org/2018/09/10/news-use-across-social-media-platforms-2018

45. Mickoleit, A (2014). Social Media Use by Governments: A Policy Primer to Discuss Trends, Identify Policy Opportunities and Guide Decision Makers. OECD Working Papers on Public Governance, No. 26: https://read.oecd-ilibrary.org/governance/social-media-use-by-governments_5jxrcmghmk0s-en#

46. Miller, Caroline (2018). Is Social Media Use Causing Depression? Childmind: https://childmind.org/article/is-social-media-use-causing-depression

47. Mitchell, Amy *et al* (2016). Many Americans Believe Fake News Is Sowing Confusion. Pew Research: https://www.journalism.org/2016/12/15/many-americans-believe-fake-news-is-sowing-confusion

48. Newman, Nic (2018). Digital News Report. Reuters Institute: https://www.digitalnewsreport.org/survey/2018/overview-key-findings-2018

49. Nonprofit Tech for Good (2019). Global NGO Technology Report 2019: https://assets-global.website-files.com/5d6eb414117b673d211598f2/5de82e1550d3804ce13ddc75_2019-Tech-Report-English.pdf

50. Ofcom (2019). Children and parents: Media use and attitudes report 2019: https://www.ofcom.org.uk/__data/assets/pdf_file/0023/190616/children-media-use-attitudes-2019-report.pdf

51. Oxford Internet Institute (2017). Stormzy 1: The Sun 0 — Three Reasons Why #GE2017 Was the Real Social Media Election: https://www.oii.ox.ac.uk/blog/stormzy-1-the-sun-0-three-reasons-why-ge2017-was-the-real-social-media-election

52. Ozimek *et al* (2017). Materialists on Facebook: The Self-Regulatory Role of Social Comparisons and the Objectification of Facebook Friends. Heliyon, vol. 3, issue 11: https://www.heliyon.com/article/e00449

53. Pandey, Manoj (2013). Governments and Social Media: https://manoj-pandey.blogspot.com/2013/09/governements-and-social-media.html

54. Pandey, Manoj (2013). Social Media: Are Governments Using Its Potential For Citizen Engagement And Socio-Economic Development?: Indian Journal of Public Administration, vol. LIX, no.2

55. Pandey, Manoj (2020). The Manual of Blogging, 2nd ed. (book): https://www.amazon.com/gp/product/B0849YHYMC

56. Perrin, Andrew (2020). 23% of users in US say social media led them to change views on an issue; some cite Black Lives Matter. Pew Research Center: https://www.pewresearch.org/fact-tank/2020/10/15/23-of-users-in-us-say-social-media-led-them-to-change-views-on-issue-some-cite-black-lives-matter

57. Primack, Brian A *et al* (2017). Use of multiple social media platforms and symptoms of depression and anxiety: A nationally-representative study among US young adults. Computers in Human Behavior, vol 69:

https://www.sciencedirect.com/science/article/pii/S0747563
216307543

58. Roth, Yoel and Pickles, Nick (2020). Updating our approach to misleading information. Twitter: https://blog.twitter.com/en_us/topics/product/2020/updating-our-approach-to-misleading-information.html

59. Seo, Hyunjin and Vu, Hong Tien (2018). Kansas University: https://news.ku.edu/2018/04/20/study-shows-changing-way-international-nonprofits-use-social-media-directly-connect

60. Shrivastava, Sambhav Kumar (2018). 40 Government Departments are using a Social Media Surveillance Tool: https://www.medianama.com/2018/09/223-40-government-departments-are-using-a-social-media-surveillance-tool-scroll-in

61. Smith, Aaron (2009). The Internet's Role in Campaign 2008. Pew Research Center: https://www.pewinternet.org/2009/04/15/the-internets-role-in-campaign-2008

62. Smith, Aaron and Anderson, Monica (2018). Social Media Use in 2018. Pew Research Center: https://www.pewinternet.org/2018/03/01/social-media-use-in-2018

63. Speciality Medical Dialogues (2019) [secondary access]. Use of Social media associated with lack of sleep in students: https://speciality.medicaldialogues.in/use-of-social-media-associated-with-lack-of-sleep-in-students

64. Sproutsocial (2017). Call-out Culture: People, Brands & the Social Media Power Struggle: https://sproutsocial.com/insights/data/q3-2017

65. Sproutsocial (2021). The Complete Guide to Social Media for Small Business. https://sproutsocial.com/social-media-for-small-business

66. Statista (2019). Distribution of worldwide social media users in 2020, by region: https://www.statista.com/statistics/295619/regional-distribution-of-social-media-users-worldwide

67. Stout, Dustin W (2019). Social Media Statistics 2019: Top Networks By the Numbers: https://dustn.tv/social-media-statistics

68. SurfShark (2021). Social media censorship tracker: https://surfshark.com/social-media-blocking

69. Top Blogs (2017). More proof of social media impacting emotional health: https://www.indiantopblogs.com/2017/03/social-media-updates.html

70. Trifonova, Viktoriya (2020). How the outbreak has changed the way we use social media. GWI: https://blog.globalwebindex.com/chart-of-the-week/social-media-amid-the-outbreak

71. Twitter (2016). Three Tips to Steer New Car Buyers' Path to Purchase: https://marketing.twitter.com/na/en/insights/three-tips-to-steer-new-car-buyers-path-to-purchase.html

72. Twitter (2019). Political Content: https://business.twitter.com/en/help/ads-policies/ads-content-policies/political-content.html

73. Wearesocial (2019). Think Forward 2020: https://wearesocial-net.s3.amazonaws.com/uk/wp-content/uploads/sites/2/2019/11/WAS_ThinkForward_2020.pdf

74. Wearesocial (2020). Digital in 2020: https://wearesocial.com/digital-2020

75. Wikipedia (2021). Programming Languages Used in Most Popular Websites: https://en.wikipedia.org/wiki/Programming_languages_used_in_most_popular_websites

76. Wikipedia (2021). Social Media: https://en.wikipedia.org/wiki/Social_media

77. Yamamoto, Masahiro *et al* (2017). U.S. Newspaper Editors' Ratings of Social Media as Influential News Sources. International Journal of Communication, vol 11: https://ijoc.org/index.php/ijoc/article/download/6386/1926

78. Young Health Movement and RSPH (2018) [secondary access]. #StateOfMind: https://www.rsph.org.uk/about-us/news/instagram-ranked-worst-for-young-people-s-mental-health.html

79. Zuckerberg, Mark (2019). A Privacy-focused Vision for Social Networking: https://www.facebook.com/notes/mark-zuckerberg/a-privacy-focused-vision-for-social-networking/10156700570096634

www.ingramcontent.com/pod-product-compliance
Lightning Source LLC
Chambersburg PA
CBHW071213240726
48654CB00009B/768